The First Amendment
and the Media
2000

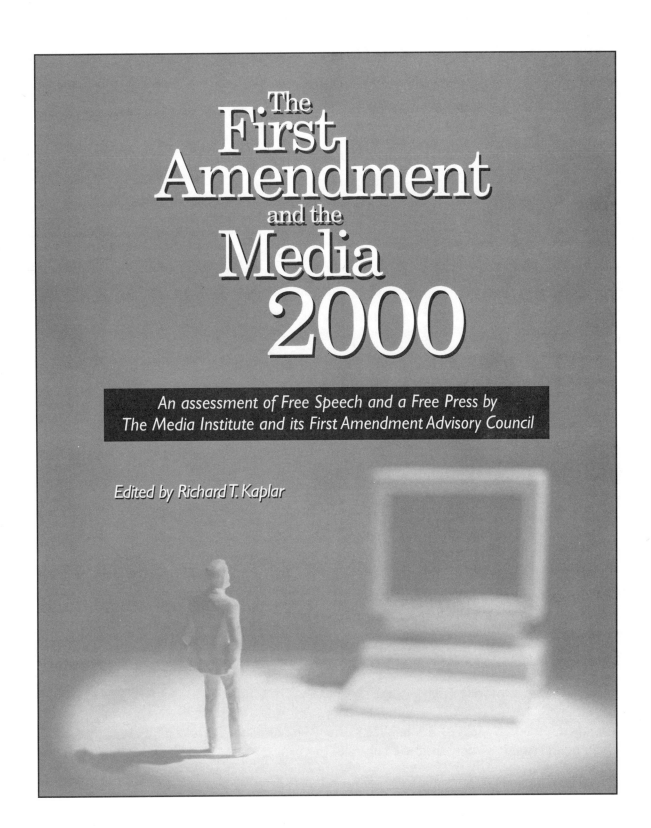

The
First
Amendment
and the
Media
2000

An assessment of Free Speech and a Free Press by
The Media Institute and its First Amendment Advisory Council

Edited by Richard T. Kaplar

The
Media
Institute

Washington, D.C.

The First Amendment and the Media - 2000
An Assessment of Free Speech and a Free Press
by The Media Institute and its
First Amendment Advisory Council

© 2000 The Media Institute

First printing March 2000.

Published by The Media Institute, Washington, D.C.

ISBN: 0-937790-64-8

Library of Congress Catalog Card Number: 00-132116

Table of Contents

Introduction
The Year of the Censor

The First Amendment seems increasingly irrelevant to growing numbers of legislators and regulators. As provocative as it may sound, this is the only conclusion one can draw after careful study of government actions affecting media speakers in 1999. We have noticed this trend for a number of years now, but it appeared firmly and regrettably entrenched as the century drew to a close. No longer is freedom of speech a bedrock principle to be defended against all onslaughts. Rather, the First Amendment has become a procedural hurdle to be overcome in pursuit of other social goals.

There was a time when legislators who stood up for free speech and free press were considered defenders of the Republic. Today the number of such defenders has dwindled. They have been replaced by a growing corps of policymakers who are considered clever if they can craft a bill or regulation that achieves its social goal while avoiding a First Amendment challenge. Moreover, speakers who claim First Amendment privilege are often characterized derisively as "hiding behind" the First Amendment, merely using it as a self-serving tool to achieve some less-than-noble purpose.

Censorship and Media Speakers

In 1999 we saw a host of actions by legislators and regulators aimed at censoring speech, particularly in the online environment. The Internet remained the frontier not only of information technology but of speech restrictions and First Amendment jurisprudence. Legislatures in Michigan and Virginia passed laws restricting Internet content available to minors. Filtering bills were passed in three states and introduced in 16 others, and several bills were introduced in Congress as well. Federal lawmakers also considered a number of anti-"spam" bills aimed at unsolicited commercial e-mail, while four states went ahead and passed such measures. Congress also passed a law censoring EPA information about potential hazards at chemical facilities. The Federal Election Commission opened an inquiry into online campaign activity, and the FBI coerced an ISP into removing a Web site about a simulated race riot in Times Square.

In the realm of traditional media, the FCC proposed rules requiring broadcasters in major markets to provide "video descriptions" of programming, and undertook an inquiry into additional public interest obligations for digital broadcasters. The Federal Trade Commission began a study of the entertainment industry's advertising to children. Congress, meanwhile, considered several bills that would censor media content deemed too violent. At the local level, a host of cities entertained measures to restrict outdoor advertising, while police in Michigan and New York appropriated journalists' photographs and used them without permission in public campaigns to help identify suspects.

The Roots of Decline

How have we come to this? Most likely it is through a convergence of factors, seemingly independent but in reality intertwined, that include a change in political philosophy, the widespread adoption of new technology, the bureaucratic mindset, and an ambivalent public.

First, policymakers have moved increasingly toward balancing and away from traditional First Amendment principles. While it is true that the First Amendment has never been an "absolute" in practice, the concept has served as an ideal, as something to strive for. Balancing, on the other hand, treats freedom of speech as just another social goal to be balanced against other goals such as tolerance, the well being of children, public safety, and public health. As Rod Smolla points out, however, "the use of the balancing approach tends to result in relatively low protection for speech" because speech becomes devalued in the process.[1]

Second, new technologies have created new opportunities for regulatory mischief. The development of a new technology disrupts the status quo by creating a regulatory void — and the new unregulated medium cries out (at least to regulators) for some type of government intervention. Should radio licensees be treated as private content providers or forced to operate as common carriers? How can cable television be regulated like broadcast TV even though it doesn't use "scarce" spectrum? These debates from earlier eras seem to pale in comparison with present efforts to regulate various aspects of the Internet. Junk e-mail ("spam"), indecency, the sale of particular products, advertising content, means of public access (filtered or unfiltered), encryption, consumer privacy — even Web surfing by public employees — have all been the subject of proposed or actual government action.

These would be perfectly understandable (if largely misguided) attempts to fill the regulatory void were it not for the fact that the Supreme Court has already established the definitive regulatory paradigm for the Internet. The Court's 1997 ruling in *Reno v. ACLU*, 521 U.S. 821 (1997), made it clear that online speech was to be accorded the same full First Amendment protections as print media. But old regulatory ways die hard and so the message has been slow to sink in, particularly among state and local policymakers. Congress has been equally unwilling to accept the new paradigm. After the Supreme Court overturned key provisions of the Communications Decency Act in *Reno v. ACLU*, lawmakers regrouped and passed another measure, the Child Online Protection Act — which also has been put on hold by a lower court and is now on appeal.

Third, policymakers are able to get away with this behavior because the American public is amazingly tolerant of incursions on First Amendment rights. The public does not hold government officials to any discernible First Amendment standard, and in fact tends to reward lawmakers (according to polling data and approval ratings) for "doing something" about perceived social problems, even at the expense of free speech. This reflects a growing and disconcerting ambivalence toward the First Amendment.

As Paul K. McMasters notes in a 1999 report by the First Amendment Center, "[Americans] are constantly reevaluating their commitment to First Amendment rights and values and rearranging their priorities, asking themselves whether life would be more civil, more orderly, less threatening if the excesses of expression were somehow subdued."[2] Indeed, that survey found that nearly one-third of respondents believe the First Amendment goes too far in the rights it guarantees, and more than half believe the press has too much freedom. Against this bleak backdrop, it is no wonder that policymakers feel free to trample the First Amendment rights of media speakers.

The First Amendment and the Courts

If there is any First Amendment respite, odds are it will be found in the courts. In 1999, for example, federal courts enjoined or dismissed three state laws restricting Internet content and issued an injunction barring enforcement of the Child Online Protection Act. The Supreme Court upheld First Amendment protection for casino gambling ads on radio and television, while lower courts ruled that the Food and Drug Administration's regulatory actions were indeed subject to First Amendment scrutiny. Other federal courts struck down state laws in Kentucky and Rhode Island that restricted the release of public records.

Even in the courts, however, First Amendment protection was not a sure thing. Results were mixed in cases involving encryption and the so-called "dirty pixels" law, reflecting the evolutionary nature of First Amendment jurisprudence in the online world. A Sixth Circuit decision weakened press rights for college journalists. And the Supreme Court issued two surprising rulings: one that upheld restrictions on the release of public court records, and another that found unconstitutional (on privacy grounds) the common newsgathering practice of "media ride-alongs" with police. Despite an imperfect record, however, the courts remained the best hope for preserving First Amendment freedoms — and provided a desperately needed check on the actions of lawmakers and regulators.

The Government's Performance

This edition marks the fourth year in which The Media Institute's First Amendment Advisory Council has graded the government's performance in protecting — or conversely, threatening — the First Amendment rights of media speakers. Members of the Council examined government actions in 43 separate issue areas grouped into four major categories: online issues; broadcasting and cable television; commercial speech; and libel law / tort actions / media restraints. Each issue area is discussed in a separate chapter of this book.

We again looked at four units of government: (1) the federal Executive Branch, comprising the Administration, federal agencies like the FDA, and regulatory commissions like the FCC and FTC; (2) the Legislative Branch, or U.S. Congress; (3) the Judicial Branch, consisting of federal district courts, appellate courts, and the U.S. Supreme Court; and (4) State and Local, which includes state courts, legislatures, regulatory agencies, and university systems, city councils, and local school boards. Some issues involved only one unit of government, such as the FCC; other issues could involve two, three, or even all four units.

Members of the Council assigned numerical grades from 50 to 100 to the relevant government units in each issue area. The grades were then tabulated, averaged, and converted to letter grades as follows:

A (90-100)	=	Superior performance in advancing or protecting First Amendment rights
B (80-89)	=	Above-average performance in advancing or protecting First Amendment rights
C (70-79)	=	Average performance; neutral impact on First Amendment
D (60-69)	=	Below-average performance; harmful to First Amendment
F (50-59)	=	Abysmal performance; actively hostile to First Amendment.

Concurrently, a committee reviewed each issue and weighted it on a scale of one to five according to its importance to the First Amendment. A Supreme Court decision with far-reaching implications would be weighted more heavily, for instance, than a narrow district court ruling. The weighted grades were used to arrive at the aggregate grades for each of the four major sections, and for the overall grades. Below are the aggregate grades, which are repeated at the beginning of each section:

	Executive	Legislative	Judicial	S & L
Online Issues	C	C	B	C-
Broadcasting and Cable	C	B-	C	C
Commercial Speech	C-	*	B	C-
Libel Law / Tort Actions / Media Restraints	C-	C	C	C-

* No Legislative Branch developments in commercial speech.

For the fourth consecutive year, the federal courts outperformed every other branch of government, although by a smaller margin than in previous years. There were no judicial home runs, but enough base hits and a few solid doubles to offset some glaring strikeouts. In fact, the performance of the Judicial Branch was about the same as last year — the gap narrowed because the other branches of government posted better grades. (Last year the Executive, Judicial, and State & Local received at least two Ds each.) The 1999 grades for State & Local may be somewhat misleading, however. These aggregate grades reflect the actions of state lawmakers and regulators, whose performance was decidedly sub-par (*e.g.*, on issues like Internet censorship and outdoor advertising bans). But the grades also reflect the decisions of state courts, some of which rendered strong First Amendment rulings (*e.g.*, in the New York *Daily News* celebrity divorce case). The resulting "Cs" do not reflect this disparity, but the differences will be readily apparent to the reader who consults relevant chapters. We averaged the grades from the four major issue categories to arrive at an overall grade for each branch of government:

Overall Grade for Protecting the First Amendment in 1999

Executive Branch	Legislative Branch	Judicial Branch	State & Local
C-	**C**	**B-**	**C-**

In 1998, by comparison, the Executive and Legislative branches each received a D+, while State & Local merited only a D- (the Judicial Branch was constant at B-). Has the situation improved? We will constrain our optimism. The Executive Branch's rise from D+ to C- is negligible (indeed inconsequential), while State & Local jumped a full grade primarily because of favorable state court decisions as discussed above — not because of any improvement by regulators. Meanwhile, Congress posted a somewhat better grade not because it did anything particularly good for the First Amendment, but merely because the year ran out before it could do anything egregiously bad.

In other words, not too much has changed. The political branches of government still pose the biggest threat to the First Amendment, and this underlying dynamic is still very much with us. It would be nice to imagine a policymaking process that truly respected and embraced the First Amendment, that gave rise to new champions of free speech from among the ranks of legislators and regulators. But as long as those branches of government can muster only average grades — grades that reflect at best a neutral stance toward the First Amendment — the prospect of such improvement seems as remote as ever. And we are left to wonder: What would our lives be like today if the Founding Fathers' feelings toward freedom of speech had been, at best, neutral?

Richard T. Kaplar
Vice President
The Media Institute
Washington, D.C.
March 2000

---

[1] Rodney A. Smolla, *The First Amendment: Freedom of Expression, Regulation of Mass Media, Freedom of Religion* (1999), at 16.

[2] First Amendment Center, *State of the First Amendment 1999* (1999), at 1.

Section I

Online Issues

ONLINE ISSUES

The Media Institute and its First Amendment Advisory Council graded the three branches of the federal government and state and local government for their support of the First Amendment regarding the above online issues as follows:

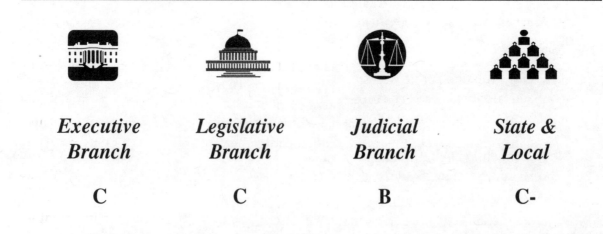

Executive Branch	*Legislative Branch*	*Judicial Branch*	*State & Local*
C	**C**	**B**	**C-**

A. Supreme Court Upholds Narrow Aspect of CDA; Federal Judge Enjoins Child Online Protection Act

Litigation continued in 1999 over the Communications Decency Act (CDA) and the Child Online Protection Act (COPA), otherwise known as "Son of CDA." The Supreme Court summarily affirmed a lower court decision that upheld, but significantly narrowed the scope of, a surviving section of the CDA that prohibited the transmission of lewd and annoying online communications. Meanwhile, a federal district court preliminarily enjoined enforcement of COPA because of its restrictive impact on online speech.

Challenges to the CDA

The CDA contained various provisions that resulted in a number of different judicial challenges. Its best known restrictions on the display or transmission of "indecent" or "patently offensive" communications online led to the Supreme Court's landmark decision in *Reno v. ACLU*, 521 U.S. 821 (1997), in which full First Amendment protections were extended to the Internet. In addition, the CDA imposed restrictions on sexually oriented cable television channels, which led to a successful challenge in *Playboy Entertainment Group, Inc. v. United States*, 30 F. Supp. 2d 702 (D. Del. 1998). The government's appeal of that three-judge district court decision was argued before the Supreme Court in 1999. *United States v. Playboy Entertainment Group, Inc.*, No. 98-1682 (argued Nov. 30, 1999).

The Supreme Court also summarily affirmed a lower court decision that had upheld the CDA's prohibition against online communications that are "lewd" and "annoying." *ApolloMedia Corp. v. Reno*, 119 S. Ct. 1450 (1999). Because the decision had the effect of upholding a section of the CDA, some published reports described it as a weakening of the precedent established in *Reno v. ACLU*. Contrary to these reports, however, the decision did not expand existing legal authority over Internet communications because the lower court decision significantly narrowed the law's scope.

The statutory provisions at issue, Sections 223(a)(1)(A) and 223(a)(2) of the CDA, prohibited online communications that are "obscene, lewd, lascivious, filthy, or indecent, with intent to annoy, abuse, threaten, or harass another person." The plaintiff in *ApolloMedia Corp.*, the publisher of a purposefully offensive Web site (www.annoy.com), argued that Sections 223(a)(1)(A) and 223(a)(2) unconstitutionally restricted its site, through which it and visitors to the site may transmit "strong views" to public officials using expression that "may be considered indecent in some communities." A three-judge district court sitting in the U.S. District Court for the Northern District of California denied the plaintiff's motion for injunctive relief and dismissed the complaint in *ApolloMedia Corp. v. Reno*, 19 F. Supp. 2d 1081 (N.D. Cal. 1998).

In response to the plaintiff's argument that the prohibition on "indecent" communications was overly broad, the government argued that the CDA provisions should be interpreted to apply only to "obscene" communications made with the "intent to annoy." The court agreed, noting that the statute should be interpreted narrowly to avoid constitutional problems.

Although a similar prohibition on "obscene, lewd, lascivious, filthy, or indecent" broadcasting had been upheld in *FCC v. Pacifica Foundation*, 438 U.S. 726 (1978), the *ApolloMedia* court did not endorse applying the broadcast indecency standard to lewd and annoying e-mail. Rather, the court distinguished the history of broadcast regulation and noted that "in the context of print media and film, the Supreme Court has read statutory 'strings of words' [that include prohibitions on filthy or indecent speech] to proscribe only material constituting obscenity within the meaning of *Miller*." *ApolloMedia Corp.*, 19 F. Supp. 2d at 1090. It then applied the same limiting construction to Internet communications.

This narrow application of the CDA provisions is consistent with the Supreme Court's treatment of other traditional means of communication, such as paper-based mail. In 1974, the Court upheld a federal law that prohibits the mailing of any "obscene, lewd, lascivious, indecent, filthy, or vile" material including "[e]very written or printed card, letter, circular, book, pamphlet, advertisement, or notice of any kind." The Court, however, found that the law could only be applied constitutionally to material found to be "obscene," and that the three-part obscenity standard articulated in *Miller v. California*, 413 U.S. 15 (1973), provided a "clarifying gloss" on the law. See *Hamling v. United States*, 418 U.S. 87 (1974). Because the transmission of obscenity online already is illegal, the CDA provisions upheld in *ApolloMedia Corp.* add little, if anything, to the law.

The Challenge to COPA

Predictably, passage of COPA led to an immediate judicial challenge. On Oct. 22, 1998, the day President Clinton signed COPA into law, the ACLU filed suit in the U.S. District Court for the Eastern District of Pennsylvania challenging the law's constitutionality. Representing various content providers on the World Wide Web, the ACLU argued that COPA infringes upon protected speech of both minors and adults, and that the law is unconstitutionally vague.

The ACLU made these arguments despite the fact that Congress drafted a law that was intended to be narrower than the CDA. For example, COPA does not apply to all sexually oriented information on the Internet, but prohibits making "any communication for commercial purposes" over the World Wide Web that "is available to any minor and that includes any material that is harmful to minors." It generally uses the three-part test for obscenity set out in *Miller v. California* as applied to minors, and thus covers material that "depicts, describes, or represents, in a manner patently offensive with respect to minors, an actual or simulated sexual act or sexual contact, an actual or simulated normal or perverted sexual act, or a lewd exhibition of the genitals or post-pubescent female breast."

COPA established criminal sanctions of a $50,000 fine and six-month imprisonment for "knowing" violations. It imposed an additional fine of $50,000 for "intentional" violations of the law, and each day of noncompliance is considered a separate violation. The law also established an additional civil fine of $50,000 for each "knowing" violation, with each day of noncompliance considered a separate violation. Like the CDA, COPA established various affirmative defenses in the event of a prosecution. If charged with a violation, a defendant may demonstrate that it restricted minors' access by use of a credit card, debit account, adult access code, adult personal identification number, digital certification, or age or other "reasonable" measure that is feasible under available technology.

In November 1998, Judge Lowell A. Reed of the U.S. District Court for the Eastern District of Pennsylvania issued a temporary restraining order blocking enforcement of COPA. *ACLU v. Reno II*, 1998 WL 813423 (E.D. Pa. 1998). Although Judge Reed acknowledged that Congress has a compelling interest in shielding children from materials that are not obscene by adult standards, he found that plaintiffs such as A Different Light Bookstore and *Salon* magazine would suffer "serious and debilitating effects" if they attempted to rely on COPA's affirmative defenses.

Without the ability to effectively use the affirmative defenses, according to the court, "COPA on its face would prohibit speech which is protected as to adults." In addition, Judge Reed found that "fears of prosecution under COPA will result in the self-censorship of [some plaintiffs'] online materials in an effort to avoid prosecution. This chilling effect will result in the censoring of constitutionally protected speech, which constitutes an irreparable harm to the plaintiffs." Ultimately, while the court agreed that the "public certainly has an interest in protecting its minors," it concluded that "the public interest is not served by the enforcement of an unconstitutional law."

This preliminary decision was reaffirmed in February 1999 when Judge Reed issued a preliminary injunction against COPA. *ACLU v. Reno II*, 31 F. Supp. 2d 473 (E.D. Pa. 1999). The decision barred the Justice Department from enforcing or prosecuting matters premised upon COPA "at any time, for any conduct that occurs while this Order is in effect." In general, the court found that the plaintiffs were likely to succeed on the merits of their constitutional claim: that the law would impose burdens on constitutionally protected speech; that it would chill online speech in general; and that the government had failed to demonstrate that COPA is the least restrictive means of serving its purpose.

Judge Reed held that, as a content-based regulation of speech, COPA is presumptively invalid and subject to strict scrutiny. The court rejected the government's assertion that the more forgiving standard for commercial speech should be applied and noted that First Amendment protection in this context "is not diminished because speakers affected by COPA may be commercial entities who speak for a profit." *Id.* at 495. Significantly, the court considered the burdens of COPA in light of "the unique factors that affect communication in the new and technology-laden medium of the Web." *Id.*

The opinion noted that any barrier erected by Web site operators and content providers to bar access to minors, even to some content, "will be a barrier that adults must cross as well." Judge Reed did not consider the economic impact of COPA on speakers (or the lack thereof) as the key issue. Instead, the court found that "First Amendment jurisprudence indicates that the relevant inquiry is determining the burden imposed on the protected speech regulated by COPA, *not* the pressure placed on the pocketbooks or bottom lines of the plaintiffs, or of other Web site operators and content providers not before the court." *Id.* (emphasis in original).

The court rejected the government's interpretation that COPA is limited only to restricting "teasers" on "porn" Web sites. It noted that COPA applies to "any Web site that contains only some harmful to minors material." If Congress had intended to adopt a narrow statute, Judge Reed suggested that it might have done so without imposing "possibly excessive and serious criminal penalties" or "without exposing speakers to prosecution and placing the burden of establishing an affirmative defense on them." *Id.* at 497.

The court also held that COPA was not the least restrictive means of protecting children. Although Judge Reed found that filtering and blocking software is not perfect, he noted that such technology "may be at least as successful as COPA would be in restricting minors' access to harmful material online without imposing the burden on constitutionally protected speech that COPA imposes on adult users or Web site operators." *Id.*

While the court found that protecting minors from sexual material online is a compelling interest, it also was "acutely conscious of its charge under the law ... not to protect the majoritarian will at the expense of stifling the rights embodied in the Constitution." It added that "perhaps we do the minors of this country harm if First Amendment protections, which they will with age inherit fully, are chipped away in the name of their protection." *Id.* at 498.

The government appealed Judge Reed's decision to the U.S. Court of Appeals for the Third Circuit. That appeal is pending.

— **Robert Corn-Revere**

B. State Regulation of Internet Challenged in Federal Courts; Fourth Circuit Rehears Public Employee Case

When it comes to regulating the content of digital communications, states don't give up easily — despite a federal court ruling in New York several years ago that such regulation burdens interstate commerce and impermissibly extends the regulating state's policies well beyond its borders. In fact, after a relatively dormant period, the past year has brought several new efforts to do precisely what New York State had been told it could not do — forbid the posting on the Internet of material that is deemed "harmful to minors." Three such laws have been under review in federal courts during 1999.

New Mexico's Statute Enjoined

New Mexico's harmful-to-minors-on-the-Internet law had been enjoined by a federal district judge in 1998. That order was promptly appealed to the U.S. Court of Appeals for the Tenth Circuit, which affirmed in early November 1999. The appellate court relied both on First Amendment and Commerce Clause grounds in striking down the New Mexico law. On the former issue, the court found that "the statute as written, like the [Communications Decency Act's indecency provisions], unconstitutionally burdens otherwise protected adult communication on the Internet." With respect to the commerce issue, the appeals court was equally critical: "[The statute] represents an attempt to regulate interstate conduct occurring outside New Mexico's borders, and is accordingly a *per se* violation of the Commerce Clause." *ACLU v. Johnson*, 194 F.3d 1149 (10th Cir. 1999).

Michigan's "Sexually Explicit" Statute

Michigan's legislature enacted a law during its 1999 session that specifically targeted the digital display or dissemination of sexually explicit material aimed at minors. Though the statute was based on a 1978 obscenity law, it replaced the term "obscene" with "sexually explicit" in provisions designed to protect young viewers and readers. The law was immediately challenged in federal court by Cyberspace Communications (the lead plaintiff) and a battery of organizations and individuals who use the Internet to distribute material arguably covered by the new provisions.

U.S. district Judge Arthur Tarnow seemed almost eager to issue a preliminary injunction. At the end of July 1999, he ruled that Michigan had breached several constitutional safeguards. Key provisions of the new law, he held, went well beyond the state's undoubted interest in protecting its young people and were not narrowly tailored to meet that interest. Moreover, the state had failed to invoke less restrictive means to achieve its goals; "the Court takes judicial notice," he remarked from the bench, "of the fact that every computer is equipped with an on/off switch."

Finally, Judge Tarnow echoed Judge Preska's earlier ruling in the New York case *American Library Association v. Pataki*, 969 F. Supp. 160 (S.D.N.Y. 1997), finding that Michigan had imposed a similarly invalid burden on interstate commerce: "A publisher of a web page cannot limit the viewing of his site to everyone in the country except for those in Michigan. The Internet has no geographic boundaries." *Cyberspace Communications v. Engler*, 55 F. Supp. 2d 737 (E.D. Mich. 1999).

Virginia's "Harmful to Juveniles" Statute

Meanwhile, as part of a major package of computer-related legislation, Virginia's General Assembly enacted a similar law. Though a conservative Republican governor opposed the bill, lawmakers at a special spring session acted to forbid Internet display of material "harmful to juveniles" if such display was for a "commercial purpose [and] in a manner whereby juveniles may examine or peruse" the material. Six months to the day from its enactment, this statute also became the focus of a federal court challenge. An eclectic group of Internet service providers, online bookstores, trade associations, and other Virginia-based information providers filed suit, alleging that the new law unduly burdened both free speech and interstate commerce.

The chairman and CEO of PSINet, one of the plaintiffs, noted the irony of such restrictive legislation in a state proclaiming itself "the cradle of the Internet." One of the individual plaintiffs, writer and lecturer Susie Bright, lamented that "all adults in Cyberspace will be reduced to sending and receiving only information which the Virginia legislature finds acceptable for juveniles" — an obvious reference to the 1957 case in which the U.S. Supreme Court used similar language to strike down a Michigan law that would in its view "reduce the adult population ... to reading only what is fit for children." Finally, the plaintiffs argued that such a law is inevitably ineffectual, in view of the vast amount of Internet material accessible to Virginia youths from sources well beyond the Old Dominion.

The suit was dismissed by a federal judge in Northern Virginia on the ground that the named defendants — the governor and the attorney general — were not the proper parties since they lacked a sufficiently close nexus to enforcement of the statute. Just before Christmas, the same group of plaintiffs refiled their complaint in federal court in Charlottesville, naming this time as defendants a group of local law enforcement officials. *PSINet, Inc. v. Chapman*, No. 99CV00111

(W.D. Va. 1999).

Fourth Circuit Reverses *Urofsky*

Virginia's governor was, of course, already in federal court on another Internet content-regulation matter. In 1996, the General Assembly had told state employees they were not to use state-owned or state-leased computers to access sexually explicit material. This law was promptly challenged by six professors at Virginia public universities, each of whom claimed valid academic reasons for using institutional computers to access explicit material. These plaintiffs also explained why the law's option to obtain a "supervisor's" permission would not meet their scholarly needs.

Federal district Judge Leonie Brinkema ruled the law violative of First Amendment freedoms on a number of grounds; it was, she concluded, both overinclusive and underinclusive, and in other respects failed to serve the asserted interests of the Commonwealth. (*Urofsky v. Allen*, 995 F. Supp. 634 (E.D. Va. 1998). That judgment was promptly appealed to the federal Fourth Circuit, which heard oral arguments in the fall of 1998.

A decision came quickly — early February 1999 — and disastrously for the plaintiffs, in *Urofsky v. Gilmore*, 167 F.3d 191 (4th Cir. 1999). A unanimous panel gave short shrift to the First Amendment claims and to Judge Brinkema's elaborate vindication of those claims. Several features saved the law — chiefly the permission option, and the fact that state employees remained free to obtain explicit imagery by using their home computers (though arguably not through university networks or servers).

Most basic, though, was the panel's conclusion that the Virginia law simply did not affect constitutionally protected public employee speech — that is, speech "on a matter of public concern." "Because plaintiffs assert only an infringement on the manner in which they perform their work as state employees," the appeals judges concluded, "they cannot demonstrate that the speech to which they claim entitlement would be made in their capacity as citizens speaking on matters of public concern."

That ruling is not, however, the last word. During the summer, the Fourth Circuit took the very unusual step of agreeing to rehear the case en banc. The full court was to have met for that purpose on Sept. 21, 1999, but adjourned that day for the funeral of a former chief judge, Sam Ervin, III. Oral argument was then rescheduled for Oct. 25, with a decision not likely until the spring or summer of 2000.

The case has never been an easy one, as the plaintiffs and their supporters are keenly aware. Most public employee expression cases deal with speaking out, not receiving information. The permission option is potentially troublesome. The Commonwealth does have an interest in making sure official business gets done on the computers it buys and leases. Yet those undoubtedly valid needs could, as Judge Brinkema ruled in the district court, be met in far less drastic ways.

Moreover, there is no evidence that viewing sexually explicit material diverts time from the Commonwealth's business to a greater degree than any of a number of other digital diversions. If the issue arose with respect to non-digital materials, the answer would be easy. If, for example, a public library told its custodians they could not use microform readers during coffee breaks to peruse old issues of *Playboy*, no court would hesitate to strike down such a ban. The issue seems more difficult, as is so often the case, mainly because the medium is unfamiliar.

— Robert M. O'Neil

C. Filtered Internet Access Looms Large in Federal and State Legislatures

Whether computers in public institutions should have filtered or unrestricted access to the Internet continued to be a major issue in 1999. Federal and state legislators took the lead in keeping the issue in the public spotlight.

Federal Legislation

Several bills were introduced (but not passed) in the 106th Congress that would have conditioned federal subsidies upon the use of Internet content filters by public schools and libraries.

Sen. John McCain (R-Ariz.) introduced the Children's Internet Protection Act, S. 97, on Jan. 19, 1999. "No issue is more important to America than protecting our children," Sen. McCain stated. The original version of the bill would have required public schools and libraries to install blocking software to prevent minors from accessing material that is "harmful to minors."

An amended version of the bill would have required public schools to certify that they had installed "technology" that filters obscenity and child pornography — categories of speech that receive no First Amendment protection. The bill would've imposed similar requirements on public libraries, depending on whether a library has one or more than one computer with Internet access. In addition, the bill provided that public schools and libraries "may" use filtering software to block material that either the school board or the library deems "inappropriate for minors." However, "inappropriate for minors" is not a recognized category of expression that is denied First Amendment protection, such as obscenity or child pornography.

Rep. Bob Franks (R-N.J.) introduced three Internet filtering bills, including the Safe Schools Internet Act of 1999, H.R. 368, and two versions of the Children's Internet Protection Act, H.R. 543 and H.R. 896. The Safe Schools Internet Act provided that public schools and libraries must install filtering software to screen out material deemed "inappropriate for minors," while the latter bills employed a less constitutionally offensive "harmful to minors" standard.

Rep. Ernest Istook (R-Okla.) introduced another filtering bill, H.R. 2560, the Child Protection Act of 1999. This bill would have required public schools and libraries to install filtering software to prevent minors from obtaining access only to obscenity and child pornography. Rep. Istook's measure also recognized that sometimes filters block constitutionally protected material. For this reason, the bill would've allowed the temporary "interruption" of filtering software to enable a minor to access material (other than obscene matter or child pornography) as long as the minor was "under the direct supervision of an adult" designated by the school or library. The Neighborhood Children's Internet Protection Act (S. 1545), introduced in the Senate by Sen. Rick Santorum (R-Pa.), contained a similar provision.

Finally, a filtering measure was added to H.R. 1501, the Juvenile Justice Reform Act of 1999. Section 1402 of the bill, like the other filtering bills, would have mandated that public schools and libraries receiving federal funds for Internet hook-ups use Internet filtering software to protect children from obscenity, child pornography, and material deemed harmful to minors.

While the standard of "inappropriate for minors" clearly is the most constitutionally offensive, opponents of mandated filtering in public institutions continue to point out that filters block some material that is constitutionally protected, thereby infringing on adults' free speech rights.

State Legislation

Filtering in public schools and libraries heated up dramatically in state legislatures across the country. Filtering bills passed in Louisiana, Michigan, and South Dakota. Filtering bills were introduced in Arkansas, California, Connecticut, Florida, Georgia, Indiana, Kansas, Massachusetts, New Mexico, Montana, North Carolina, New Jersey, New Mexico, New York, Pennsylvania, and Virginia.

The Arizona measure, signed by the governor in April 1999, provides that public schools install blocking software that will prevent minors from accessing material "harmful to minors." The Arizona law provides that public libraries must either install blocking software to prevent minors from accessing material harmful to minors or develop "a policy that establishes measures to restrict minors from gaining computer access to material that is harmful to minors."

The Louisiana bill, signed by the governor in July, requires public elementary and secondary schools to adopt policies monitoring student access to material "reasonably believed" to be obscenity, child pornography, "conducive to the creation of a hostile or dangerous school environment," "pervasively vulgar," or "excessively violent or sexually harassing in the school environment." The bill states that any such policy shall include the use of "computer-related technology ... designed to block access or exposure to any harmful material." The law does not prevent students from having unrestricted Internet access for "legitimate scientific or educational purposes."

The Michigan law, signed by the governor in June, provides that libraries "may" restrict minors' access to certain material on the Internet "by making available, to individuals of any age, one or more terminals that are restricted from receiving obscene matter or sexually explicit matter that is harmful to minors." At the same time, libraries must make available "to individuals 18 years of age or older or minors who are accompanied by their parent or guardian, one or more terminals that are not restricted from receiving any material."

The new law, which went into effect Aug. 1, 1999, has kept at least one Michigan public library from installing filtering software on all computers for all terminals. The Michigan chapter of the American Civil Liberties Union indicated in Fall 1999 that it may challenge the policy. See David Hudson, "Michigan ACLU will likely challenge library's Internet filtering policy," *free! The Freedom Forum Online*, Aug. 13, 1999 <www.freedom forum.org/speech/8/13michigan. asp>. A similar policy was struck down by a federal court in *Mainstream Loudoun v. Board of Trustees of the Loudoun County Public Library* (see below).

The South Dakota bill, signed by the governor in March, would require public schools (including state-owned universities) and public libraries to protect minors from obscene materials on the Internet. See David Hudson, "South Dakota to require public schools, universities to filter Internet access," *free! The Freedom Forum Online*, March 11, 1999 <www.freedom forum.org/speech/1999/3/11southdakota.asp>. Under the bill, public schools or libraries could accomplish their goal of protecting minors from obscene material through the use of filters or implementation of local policies to restrict minors' access to obscene materials.

Numerous other bills were introduced in other states. Many of the bills will be automatically carried over to the start of the next legislative session while others will have to be re-introduced. The bills vary as to whether they:

* apply to public schools or libraries or both;
* mandate filtering or a choice between filtering and some other policy designed to prevent minors from accessing harmful material; and
* restrict access to obscenity, child pornography, material deemed "harmful to minors," or material deemed "inappropriate for minors."

Filtering Cases

In the seminal filtering case *Mainstream Loudoun v. Board of Trustees of the Loudoun County Public Library*, 24 F. Supp. 2d 552 (E.D. Va. 1998), federal district court Judge Leonie Brinkema ruled that the county's Internet access policy for the public library was unconstitutional. The policy required the filter "X-Stop" to be installed on all computer terminals for all patrons. Brinkema said the policy "offends the guarantee of free speech in the First Amendment" in a November 1998 ruling.

In April 1999, the board, which had changed membership since the adoption of the filtering policy, decided not to appeal Judge Brinkema's decision to the U.S. Court of Appeals for the Fourth Circuit. See David Hudson, "Library board won't appeal court decision barring mandatory filtering," *free! The Freedom Forum Online*, April 22, 1999 <www.freedomforum.org/ speech/ 1999/4/22loudoun.asp>.

The other major Internet filtering case, *Kathleen R. v. City of Livermore*, Case No. V-015266-4 (Super. Ct., Alameda County), is on appeal before a California appeals court. Kathleen R. sued the city of Livermore, contending that the city must install filtering software to protect minors from harmful material on the Internet.

Kathleen R. sued after her minor son downloaded scores of pornographic pictures from the city library and distributed them at school. In October 1998, a California state judge ruled that Section 230c(1) of the Communications Decency Act of 1996 provides immunity to the library. That section says that "[n]o provider or user of an interactive computer service shall be treated as the publisher or speaker of any information provided by another information content provider."

Groups on both sides of the filtering debate have weighed in with *amicus* briefs. The American Civil Liberties Union and People for the American Way have filed a brief supporting the lower court ruling, while Enough Is Enough and the American Family Association have indicated they will file a brief in support of Kathleen R. Michael Millen, attorney for Kathleen R., told the author that he does not expect a hearing before the California appeals court until "late 2000."

— **David L. Hudson, Jr.**

D. Courts, Administration, Congress Take Steps Toward Protecting Encrypted Speech

"Encryption" is the ability to encode information sent over computer networks to make it readable only by the intended receiver. Encryption was originally the exclusive province of military and intelligence services, and its dissemination was tightly controlled for national security reasons. Today, however, encryption is widely used to protect privacy and proprietary information stored or transmitted electronically. A wide variety of everyday products, from cell phones to Web browsers, have encryption features built in.

Certain "strong" encryption — truly effective in ensuring the privacy of electronic communications — cannot legally be exported or even published on the Internet because of concerns that it may be used to shield criminal and terrorist activities. This prohibition against publishing is, of course, a classic prior restraint. As more communications occur electronically, privacy advocates and the information technology industry have become convinced that effective encryption is necessary both to ensure that sensitive communications stay private and to facilitate the growth of electronic commerce.

Nonetheless, the U.S. government has been slow to retreat from its traditional policies restricting the export of encryption technologies outside the United States. Law enforcement and national security agencies are concerned that criminals and terrorists will use encryption themselves to evade detection or to hide evidence. The government's policies have been under strong pressure from information technology vendors and users, however, and have also suffered setbacks in litigation with academic cryptographers. Bills have also been introduced in Congress that would substantially liberalize U.S. export controls on encryption, and have garnered significant support in both chambers.

In 1999, a panel of the U.S. Court of Appeals for the Ninth Circuit held, in strong and sweeping language, that restrictions on publishing encryption code violate the First Amendment. However, that panel withdrew its opinion pending a petition for rehearing by the entire Ninth Circuit. In late 1999 the Clinton Administration announced new policies that should substantially reduce the export restrictions on many forms of strong encryption. On the congressional front, several bills to liberalize controls on encryption were introduced but failed to pass Congress.

The Courts: First Amendment Challenges to Encryption Regulations

The long-standing restrictions on encryption source code have also been under attack in the courts on constitutional grounds. In three separate lawsuits, academic cryptographers have argued that the requirement to obtain a government license before publishing encryption source code on the Internet or by other electronic means is nothing more than a prior restraint on free speech contrary to the First Amendment. These scientists maintain that source code is a medium of communication, in fact the preferred medium for communication among computer scientists, and is thus protected speech. The government has defended the regulations by maintaining that source code is functional, not speech, and that it is regulated for what it does and not for any ideas it may communicate.

The results so far have been mixed. The district court in the *Bernstein* case held that source code was protected speech and struck down the export regulations as an unconstitutional prior restraint. *Bernstein v. Department of State*, 922 F. Supp. 1426 (N.D. Cal. 1996); 945 F. Supp. 1279 (N.D. Cal. 1996); 974 F. Supp. 1288 (N.D. Cal. 1997). A Ninth Circuit panel upheld the district court (see 176 F.3d 1132 (9th Cir. 1999)), but that opinion has been withdrawn subject to further proceedings, perhaps at the district court. The district courts in the *Karn* and *Junger* cases rejected the professors' challenges and upheld the government's regulations. *Junger v. Daley*, 8 F. Supp. 2d 709 (N.D. Ohio 1998); *Karn v. Department of State*, 925 F. Supp. 1, 9-10 (D.D.C. 1996). The *Karn* case was appealed to the D.C. Circuit, then remanded to the district court (and a new judge) for further proceedings. The *Junger* case is on appeal to the Sixth Circuit.

New encryption regulations adopted in January 2000 may have substantial impact on the claims at issue in these cases. The regulations include a narrow exception that would allow encryption source code to be exported without licensing to most destinations, provided that (1) it is or will be released publicly; (2) it is not subject to any "proprietary commercial agreement or restriction"; and (3) the exporter (publisher) of the source code notifies the Commerce Department prior to export or publication, and provides the Commerce Department with a copy of the code or identifies the URL at which it can be found. That might seem to moot the claims of these professors, who wish to post source code publicly on the Internet and have not imposed any proprietary restrictions on it.

However, the exception would not permit export to terrorist-supporting countries or their nationals, which would seem, as a practical matter, to preclude Internet publication. In addition, the requirements for notice and disclosure to the government prior to publication are unusual, to say the least, and might not pass constitutional muster.

Executive Branch Actions: Improved Regulations

Export controls over cryptographic software were significantly revised in January 2000 and will be reviewed in detail in next year's edition of this publication. Traditionally, cryptographic products and software have been governed by export licensing requirements. The strength of encryption products is typically measured by the key length, or number of "bits" in the encryption key, which is a string of randomly generated digits used to encrypt or decrypt information. Although generally accepted security standards today demand 128-bit encryption for most applications, Commerce Department regulations in effect prior to January 2000 effectively set up a 56-bit upper limit for general export to destinations other than Canada. Exports of stronger encryption products, with some exceptions, generally required explicit prior Commerce Department licensing. ("Export" for this purpose includes posting software on the Internet and release of source code in electronic form to foreign nationals in the United States or elsewhere. In addition, re-exports of encryption products — that is, exports of U.S.-origin encryption from one foreign country to another — were subject to the same licensing requirements.)

The regulations established several narrow but important exceptions to the requirement for licensing prior to export: First, exports or re-exports could be made to almost any destination (other than a few countries claimed to support terrorism) without a license if they fell within one of the following three categories:

- Encryption products that use key lengths up to 56 bits.
- Encryption products of any strength (*i.e.*, greater than 56 bits) exported to subsidiaries of U.S. companies for internal company proprietary use.
- Encryption products of any strength specifically designed and limited for financial transactions.

Second, exports or re-exports of encryption products with any strength or key length could be made to certain defined end-users located in one of 45 specified countries:

- To banks and financial institutions, including insurance companies, formed and regulated in one of the specified 45 countries, and to their branches located anywhere in the world except the designated terrorist countries.
- To civilian health and medical service providers, including organizations that reimburse health costs.
- To online merchants for electronic commerce (*e.g.*, the Internet) to purchase or sell goods or software.

To be eligible for export or re-export under any of these exceptions, the products (hardware and software) had to be submitted to the Commerce Department by the manufacturer or producer for a one-time technical review. In addition, exporters had to file periodic reports for some categories of export identifying the end-users who received the product. It was possible to secure licensing for exports that did not qualify for one of the exceptions. The Commerce Department granted a number of licenses for specific exports of strong encryption to reliable users in developed countries, and said it would give favorable consideration to export requests from strategic business partners of U.S. companies.

In September 1999, the Clinton Administration announced it would issue new regulations that would substantially reduce or even eliminate many restrictions on encryption exports. Not surprisingly, perhaps, crafting specific regulatory language to carry out that broad policy announcement proved more difficult and more contentious than expected. The new regulations were issued in mid-January 2000.

The September announcement promised that the new regulations would have the following features:

- The threshold for general export without prior licensing will be raised from 56 bits to 64 bits.
- Encryption products that qualify as "retail" products may be exported with any strength encryption to any user or destination (except the terrorist-supporting countries).
- "Non-retail" products may be exported with any strength encryption to non-government entities (except in terrorist-supporting countries). Exports of non-retail encryption stronger than 64 bits to government-owned entities will require specific licensing, however.
- Exporters will be required to make periodic post-export reports concerning the destination and other details for exports of encryption greater than 64 bits.
- As before, all encryption products must be submitted to the Commerce Department for a one-time technical review, which will presumably determine, among other things, whether the product qualifies as "retail" or "non-retail."

Exactly how these regulations will be applied is still uncertain. For instance, initial drafts of the regulations apparently suggested that software delivered over the Internet would not meet the definition of "retail," to the obvious consternation of the e-commerce community. In the same vein, some have complained that the definition of "government entities" may preclude exports to a number of national telecommunications companies and other significant business enterprises owned, in whole or in part, by governments.

The initial drafts have also been subject to criticism because they apparently suggested that products with "open cryptographic interfaces" would not be eligible for export without a license under any of the categories described above. That would apparently mean that software with strong encryption could be exported without a license but software that has no encryption features itself, but merely has an interface that enables encryption from another source, would require a license before export.

Another issue of controversy has been Internet publication or other dissemination of "open source" software. The September announcement indicated the new rules would apply only to object code software and that strict licensing requirements would still apply to source code. That seemed to ignore the growing importance of "open source" software, for which developers publish all of the source code to the world, so that others can build upon it and improve it as well as develop compatible products. Initial drafts attempted to carve out an exception that would authorize Internet posting of noncommercial source code by academics and others, but many have complained that it is not broad enough to allow effective "open source" development.

Congress: Support for Liberalization, but No Bills Passed

Several bills were introduced in Congress to liberalize encryption regulations in 1999, but none passed. For example, the Technology Committee of the House Science Committee approved by voice vote the Computer Security Enhancement Act of 1999 (H.R. 2413), sponsored by Rep. Jim Sensenbrenner (R-Wis.). Portions of this bill would have liberalized encryption regulations. Although the bill did not pass Congress, it and other legislative efforts are credited with creating incentives for the Administration to liberalize its encryption regulations.

— Kurt Wimmer

E. Four States Adopt Anti-'Spam' Laws; Congress Ponders E-Mail Bills While AOL Wins Court Challenge

The issue of unsolicited electronic mail, or "spam," is a volatile one. On one hand, Internet users — and the Internet service providers (ISPs) that deliver e-mail to them — despise spam. From the perspective of users, it clogs e-mail boxes and brings content they find inappropriate (particularly advertisements for adult Web sites) into their homes. From the ISPs' perspective, spam represents a drain on the Internet system.

Bulk, unsolicited e-mail messages routinely overload ISPs' servers (hundreds of GTE business customers lost their Internet service briefly in December 1999 because of a spam-generated overload). Unlike telemarketers or junk mailers, who pay phone and mail costs, spammers can send millions of e-mail messages at virtually no cost. But the cost of delivering millions of bulk e-mail messages to the system and to users can be great.

On the other hand, of course, even unsolicited e-mail messages constitute speech. A number of bills passed this year by state legislatures attempt broadly to ban spam without recognizing the potential First Amendment values implicated by flat bans on speech. Others attempt to limit their constitutional liability by requiring labeling or penalizing only false and deceptive commercial e-mail.

Federal Legislative Efforts

Several proposals similar to the state measures are pending before Congress, which has yet to pass legislation concerning unsolicited e-mail. On Oct. 19, 1999, Rep. Heather Wilson (R-N.M.) introduced the latest e-mail bill, the Unsolicited Electronic Mail Act of 1999 (H.R. 3113).

Legislators discussed four of these House proposals in a hearing before the House Commerce Committee's Subcommittee on Telecommunications, Trade, and Consumer Protection on Nov. 3. At these hearings, a Federal Trade Commission official warned that the proliferation of spam threatens consumer confidence in electronic commerce. Eileen Harrington of the FTC's Bureau of Consumer Protection said that "[n]ot all unsolicited commercial e-mail is fraudulent, but fraud operators — often among the first to exploit any technological innovation — have seized on the Internet's capacity to reach literally millions of consumers quickly and at a low cost."

Other federal legislation includes the Inbox Privacy Act (S. 759), introduced in March 1999 by Sens. Frank Murkowski (R-Alaska) and Robert Torricelli (D-N.J.). This act would require e-mail marketers to include their correct name, physical address, Internet address, and telephone number in all bulk unsolicited e-mail. It also would require marketers to honor "no spam" notices posted by consumers, domain name users, and ISPs.

The E-Mail User Protection Act, introduced in May 1999 by Rep. Gene Green (R-Texas), is similar in its terms to the Inbox Privacy Act. It also would make it illegal to use, create, sell, or distribute software primarily designed to generate false addresses on bulk e-mail messages. Finally, the "Can Spam Act" was introduced by Rep. Gary Miller (R-Calif.) in June 1999. This act would create a civil cause of action for ISPs that suffer damages due to mass unsolicited e-mail, with damages of up to $25,000 per day or $50 per message. It also would create criminal penalties for the unauthorized use of domain names, another tactic often used by spammers.

State Legislation

Most of the specific legislation against unsolicited e-mail has been enacted on the state front. For example, on Jan. 1, 1999, California's anti-spam laws went into effect. These laws make it a crime to use a California computer network to send advertisements by e-mail that violate the policies of an ISP. They also require the labeling of e-mail advertisements on the subject line of each e-mail.

On March 30, 1999, Virginia followed suit. Under the new Virginia Computer Crimes Act, ordinary spamming is a misdemeanor punishable by a fine of up to $500. "Malicious" spamming, defined as spam that causes more than $2,500 in losses, constitutes a felony that can be punished by up to five years in prison. The Virginia law grants both Internet users and ISPs the right to sue spammers for damages ranging from $10 per illegal message to $25,000 per day, whichever is greater. The Virginia Act focuses on e-mail that "falsifies" or "forges" the identity of the sender, a common practice among spammers. This focus on "false" identities also may assist the law in withstanding constitutional challenge.

Similarly, amendments to Delaware's "Misuse of Computer Information" statute were signed into law on July 2, 1999. These amendments make it illegal to send, intentionally or "recklessly," any unsolicited bulk commercial e-mail without the authorization of the recipients. The law excludes e-mail sent between individuals, from an organization to its members, in response to a request, or pursuant to an existing business relationship. It also prohibits falsifying transmission information on e-mail messages, the sale of software to facilitate spamming, and failing to stop sending e-mail when requested.

Finally, Illinois signed into law the "Illinois Electronic Mail Act," which prohibits Illinois businesses or individuals from sending unsolicited e-mail without authorization when any element of the transmission path of the message is falsified or when the subject line contains false or misleading information. Violations will be punished as consumer fraud or deceptive trade practices.

Federal and State Court Litigation

Although civil liberties groups have objected to restrictions on spam on First Amendment grounds, most state litigation against alleged spammers to date has been brought by ISPs.

For example, on Dec. 14, 1999, a magistrate judge of the U.S. District Court for the Southern District of New York ruled in favor of America Online, Inc. in its claim that the defendant's unauthorized sending of unsolicited commercial e-mail to AOL subscribers violated the federal computer fraud statute, 18 U.S.C. Sec. 1030. The court reasoned that the defendant's actions constituted the misappropriation of services that could have been sold to a paying advertiser. The court refused to apply the law of any state except Virginia, where AOL resides, and found that Virginia's Computer Crimes Act could not be applied retroactively.

Other cases in the state courts are pending. Web site and free e-mail service Yahoo! Inc. filed suit against two companies in California in April 1999, claiming that they forged Yahoo! e-mail addresses to send marketing materials. The suit alleges forgery and trademark infringement. In another action, Connect Northwest Internet Services, an ISP based in Washington State, filed suit against CTX Mortgage Company in May 1999, alleging that CTX violated Washington's anti-spam law. The suit claims that on April 8, thousands of unsolicited messages from CTX flooded and crashed Connect Northwest's e-mail server. Connect Northwest is seeking $5.8 million in damages.

International Efforts to Limit Spam

It is interesting to note that efforts to limit spam are not, by any means, limited to the United States. Two German Internet journals, *c't* and *politik-digital*, have asked citizens of European Union countries to sign a petition calling on the European Parliament to support the introduction of EU-level legislation against spam. Various members of the Parliament have expressed support for the German petition. In August 1999, the EU issued a call for proposals to assess data privacy issues raised by unsolicited e-mail advertising.

A number of court actions have been taken against spammers internationally as well. In March 1999, a Toronto-based ISP, I.D. Internet Direct, sued an alleged spammer. The court ultimately decided in I.D. Internet's favor and entered an injunction against the spammer using the ISP's facilities and required him to pay its legal fees. Another Toronto ISP, Nexx Online, terminated service to a customer that sent 200,000 unsolicited commercial e-mails per day. In response to a suit by the spammer claiming breach of contract, the Ontario Superior Court held that spamming violated principles of "netiquette" with which the spammer had agreed to comply when signing up for the ISP's service.

A German court in January 1999 held that German law provides a right to injunctive relief and damages to German citizens damaged by unsolicited commercial communications, including e-mail. And in Hong Kong, a 25-year-old computer systems administrator was tried on criminal charges stemming from his e-mail to 5,000 Internet users. The court in August 1999 acquitted the defendant because of a lack of "dishonest intent," and this result led to calls to the Hong Kong government to pass legislation banning spam.

— Kurt Wimmer

F. First, Eleventh Circuits Uphold 'Dirty Pixels' Law While Ninth Circuit Invalidates Key Portions

In *United States v. Hilton*, 999 F. Supp. 131 (D. Me. 1998), the federal district court in Maine struck down the so-called "Dirty Pixels" law, the Child Pornography Prevention Act of 1996, 18 U.S.C. Sec. 2252A (CPPA). The district court said in its 1998 ruling that the CPPA is content neutral, but nevertheless invalidated the statute as both impermissibly vague and overbroad. (See *The First Amendment and the Media - 1999*.)

In January 1999, however, the U.S. Court of Appeals for the First Circuit held that the district court had mistaken the CPPA for a content-neutral law — but the First Circuit then unanimously reversed by construing the law in such a way that it survived the facial constitutional challenge presented. *United States v. Hilton*, 167 F.3d 61 (1st Cir. 1999), *cert. denied*, 1999 U.S. LEXIS 5406 (Oct. 4, 1999). In November, the Eleventh Circuit also held that the CPPA is not facially invalid, nor is it overbroad or vague. *United States v. Acheson*, 195 F.3d 645 (11th Cir. 1999). But in December, a split panel of the Ninth Circuit struck down key portions of the Act, setting the stage for likely Supreme Court review next year. *The Free Speech Coalition v. Reno*, 25 Media L. Rep. 2305 (N.D. Cal. Aug. 12, 1997) (not reported in F. Supp.), *aff'd in part, rev'd in part*, ___ F.3d. ___ , 1999 WL 1206649 (9th Cir. 1999).

Background

In *New York v. Ferber*, 458 U.S. 747 (1982), the Court created a new category of expression, child pornography, outside the protection of the First Amendment in sustaining a New York law prohibiting the distribution of material depicting children engaged in sexual conduct, even if this material would not be obscene under the standard of *Miller v. California*, 413 U.S. 15 (1973). But the Court's opinion made it clear that the concern was to limit the sexual exploitation and abuse of actual children in either the production of the material or the distribution of a permanent, visible record of the children's participation.

The Court noted that individuals over the statutory age who look younger, or other forms of simulation, could be used to create an illusion, and no particular literary theme or portrayal of sexual activity that does not use real children could be censored under the state statute. *Ferber*, 458 U.S. at 758-64. In *Osborne v. Ohio*, 495 U.S. 103 (1990), a majority of the Court, over a dissent by Justice Brennan, extended the rationale of *Ferber* by allowing a state to make unlawful the mere possession of child pornography.

In 1996, however, Congress enacted the CPPA to attack computerized or "virtual" child pornography as the latest in a long series of successively more stringent regulations of child pornography. See *The Free Speech Coalition v. Reno*, 1999 WL 1206649 at *2-*4, for a survey of this legislative progression. The CPPA now criminalizes the reproduction, possession, sale, or distribution of visual images depicting minors or those who "appear to be" minors engaging in sexually explicit conduct, or such images that are distributed or advertised in such a manner as to "convey the impression" that the depiction portrays a minor. Congress deliberately designed these prohibitions to reach materials produced — by computer, for example — without the involvement of any actual children, well beyond the concern for this aspect of child abuse or exploitation central to the *Ferber* opinion.

Prior to the CPPA, "the actual participation and abuse of [real] children in the production or dissemination of pornography involving minors was the *sine qua non* of the regulating scheme." *The Free Speech Coalition* at *4. Now, Congress's concern was that the proliferating volume of computerized child pornography could "stimulate or whet" the sexual appetites of child molesters and pedophiles who then use virtual pornography in the "grooming process" to seduce or entice actual children into participating in sexual activity by breaking down their natural inhibitions. Congress also worried that the privacy of actual children was being invaded when their innocuous images were altered or morphed to create sexually explicit pictures. See *Hilton*, 167 F.3d at 66-67.

United States v. Hilton

Hilton was indicted for criminal possession of computer disks containing images of child pornography. He moved to dismiss the indictment, mounting solely a facial attack on the CPPA by arguing it was unconstitutionally vague and overbroad. The district court found that the statute is a content-neutral time, place, or manner regulation "designed to ameliorate significant harmful secondary effects of the protected speech rather than suppress the speech itself." *Hilton*, 999 F. Supp. at 134. Nonetheless, the court found the "appears to be ... a minor" language both vague and overbroad and so invalidated the law and dismissed the indictment.

On the government's appeal, the court of appeals first corrected the district court's mistake in construing the CPPA as content neutral. Rather, the law is directed at the impact of the speech on its viewers and singles out and bans a type of expression, child pornography, based on its content. As such, it is a "quintessential content-specific statute." *Hilton*, 167 F.3d at 68-69.

But then the First Circuit reviewed *Ferber* and *Osborne* and concluded that, where child pornography is concerned, legislatures have greater leeway to regulate sexual depictions of children through adequately defined legislative terms, and considerations beyond the direct abuse of actual children may qualify as compelling government objectives.

The CPPA is not constitutionally overbroad, according to the First Circuit, because the legislative record shows that the language "appears to be ... a minor" must be construed narrowly to apply only to "a specific subset of visual images — those which are easily mistaken for that of real children." *Id.* at 72. With this limitation, "it is a logical and permissible extension of the rationales in *Ferber* and *Osborne* to allow the regulation of sexual materials that appear to be of children but did not, in fact, involve the use of live children in their production." *Id.* at 73.

The court did note that a simulated depiction that is a serious contribution to art or science — such as using a youthful-looking adult to portray Lolita in a sexual encounter — should be able to invoke "an affirmative First Amendment defense ... although we need not define now its precise dimensions. *Id.* at 74. That some unconstitutional convictions might have to be reversed was no reason for the court to invalidate the statute *in toto*.

The court also ruled the CPPA is not unconstitutionally vague because the "appears to be ... a minor" requirement is to be judged on an objective standard — would a reasonable, unsuspecting viewer consider the depiction to be of an actual underage individual — and is subject to a scienter requirement." *Id.* at 74. The court offered some examples of evidence that could be used to establish the apparent age of the person depicted. Also, in some circumstances a distributor (but not a possessor) of child pornography will have available the defense that an actual adult was used in the production if the defendant did nothing in promoting the material to convey the impression that the actor was a minor.

United States v. Acheson

The defendant in *Acheson* pled guilty to violating the CPPA, admitting the truthfulness of the government's proffer, but reserving the right to challenge the constitutionality of the act. Again the challenge focused on the "appears to be ... a minor" language. In accord with *Hilton*, the defendant's facial attack failed because, although the court acknowledged the CPPA as a content-based restriction on speech, Congress is entitled to greater leeway in regulating child pornography, an unprotected category of expression.

Moreover, "[g]iven the lack of any substantial overbreadth in light of the statute's legitimate sweep," the CPPA is not impermissibly overbroad. *Acheson*, 195 F.3d at 652. The CPPA is not void for vagueness because a "reasonable person is [put] on notice that possessing images appearing to be children engaged in sexually explicit conduct is illegal," and "[t]he physical characteristics of the person depicted in the image go a long way towards determining whether the person appears to be a minor." *Id.* at 652-53. Finally, the scienter requirements in the CPPA provide adequate protection against improper or arbitrary enforcement.

The Free Speech Coalition v. Reno

In *The Free Speech Coalition*, a trade association of businesses involved in the production and distribution of "adult-oriented materials" brought a pre-enforcement challenge to portions of the CPPA seeking declaratory and injunctive relief. The district court, like the district court in *Hilton*, found the CPPA to be content neutral, aimed at the secondary effects of child pornography, and neither unconstitutionally overbroad nor vague. The Ninth Circuit, however, followed the First Circuit in *Hilton* insofar as treating the Act as a content-based restriction on speech that the government must show is narrowly tailored to serve a compelling interest.

But the government could not provide a compelling interest to the extent the CPPA's definition of child pornography includes visual depictions that "appear" to be of minors or that "convey" the impression that a minor is engaging in sexually explicit conduct. The Act thus criminalizes "the use of fictional images that involve no human being ... [or that are] entirely the product of the mind." *The Free Speech Coalition*, 1999 WL 1206649 at *7. The Act therefore is a "significant departure from *Ferber*" whose "focus of analysis is on the harm to the children actually used in the production of the materials." *Id.*

Here the majority criticized the dissent's position based on a secondary effects justification and dicta from *Osborne*. The majority noted that *Osborne* involved real children, and "[p]rotecting harm to real children is the point that constitutionally limits the power of Congress to ban some forms of expression." *Id.* at *9 n.7. The majority relied on a Seventh Circuit opinion for the proposition that the effects of expression — especially representations of virtual reality — on the minds of others cannot be enough to justify government regulation. *American Booksellers Association, Inc. v. Hudnut*, 771 F.2d 323 (7th Cir. 1985), *aff'd*, 475 U.S. 1001 (1986) (mem.) (invalidating a city ordinance prohibiting pornography that portrays women submissively or in a degrading manner). Such a secondary effects argument based on how speech affects the listener or viewer "would turn First Amendment jurisprudence on its head." *The Free Speech Coalition*,1999 WL 1206649 at *10. But a "critical ingredient" of the majority's analysis was the absence of any factual studies establishing a link between computer-generated child pornography and the subsequent sexual abuse of children. *Id.* at *9.

The majority also found the statutory phrases "appears to be a minor" and "convey[s] the impression" to be unconstitutionally vague and overbroad. These phrases are "highly subjective ... [t]here is no explicit standard as to what the phrases mean." *Id.* at *11. This could allow law enforcement officials to exercise their discretion in an arbitrary and discriminatory fashion. But these defects are severable from the overall statute, and the court made clear that the CPPA may be enforced as to morphed computer images of an identifiable child because this involves the potential for harm to a real child.

The sharp division among several circuit courts on an issue of the CPPA's constitutionality under the First Amendment will almost surely prompt Supreme Court review of this difficult and controversial issue next term.

— Laurence H. Winer

G. Ban on Bombmaking Information Rides Again as Congress Weighs Juvenile Justice Bill

Since 1995 Congress has considered legislation to restrict the dissemination of bombmaking information on the Internet. In past years, it has resisted the impulse to enact such legislation. See "Congress again kills legislation to restrict the dissemination of bombmaking information," *The First Amendment and the Media - 1998*, at 29-31. But in 1999, in the wake of the Littleton, Colo., school shooting tragedy, the legislation was revived and appears very likely to pass.

The provision was added as an amendment to the Violent and Repeat Juvenile Offender Accountability and Rehabilitation Act of 1999 (the "Juvenile Justice Bill"), introduced in the Senate by Sen. Orrin G. Hatch (R-Utah) in response to youth violence in schools. The omnibus legislation contains a wide range of initiatives designed to combat youth violence. After Littleton, Sen. Dianne Feinstein (D-Calif.), the sponsor of previous attempts to restrict bombmaking information, introduced Amendment 353, which provides in relevant part:

> It shall be unlawful for any person to teach or demonstrate the making of explosive materials, or to distribute by any means information pertaining to, in whole or in part, the manufacture of explosive materials, if the person intends or knows that such explosive materials or information will be used for, or in furtherance of, an activity that constitutes a Federal criminal offense or a criminal purpose affecting interstate commerce.

Amendment 353 was approved by the Senate on May 18, 1999 by a vote of 85-13. See 145 Cong. Rec. S5194 (daily ed. May 13, 1999). The Senate approved the legislation two days later by a vote of 73-25. See 145 Cong. Rec. S5725 (daily ed. May 20, 1999). At the end of 1999, the Juvenile Justice bill had been referred to a conference committee to reconcile the Senate bill with the House version, H.R. 1501. The House bill would amend the criminal code to prohibit making, printing, or publishing a notice or advertisement by computer seeking to distribute a firearm or explosive in violation of the Brady Act or other federal firearms provisions.

More Symbolic Than Substantive

If the Feinstein amendment is adopted as part of a final Juvenile Justice bill, it will represent the culmination of five years of effort to adopt restrictions on bombmaking information. Yet, ironically, its adoption would be more symbolic than substantive, since it would largely duplicate existing federal laws. This is because the thrust of the proposed restrictions were narrowed following a 1997 report to Congress by the Department of Justice. See *Report on the Availability of Bombmaking Information, the Extent to Which Its Dissemination Is Controlled by Federal Law, and the Extent to Which Such Dissemination May Be Subject to Regulation Consistent With the First Amendment to the United States Constitution* (April 1997), at 5 ("DOJ Bombmaking Report"). In the place of an earlier proposal by Sen. Feinstein, Congress had directed the attorney general to study the availability of bombmaking information in any medium (including print, electronic, or film) and to report on the need for new legislation. See Antiterrorism and Effective Death Penalty Act of 1996, Pub. L. No. 104-132, Sec. 709(a), 110 Stat. 1214, 1297 (1996).

In its resulting report, the Department of Justice concluded that a broad prohibition on Internet communication would be constitutionally suspect because it would "deter altogether the dissemination of information." The DOJ Bombmaking Report applied the same First Amendment standards to the Internet that apply to printed materials and concluded that any proposed law must be tailored to restrict particular persons who, the sender of information believes, are likely to use bombmaking information for criminal purposes. DOJ Bombmaking Report, at 49-50. Under this analysis, the government could not simply ban the publication of bombmaking materials on the Internet. The Department recommended specific changes to narrow and clarify the proposed legislation. Based on the Report, Sen. Feinstein introduced a narrower version of the legislation, which applied to dissemination of bombmaking information "by any means," and required a showing that the speaker knows or intends that the information will be used to commit a crime.

If adopted as narrowed, the legislation will add little, if anything, to existing law. Federal law already prohibits the dissemination or teaching of bombmaking information (1) as part of an agreement to commit a federal crime, 18 U.S.C. Sec. 373; (2) for the specific purpose of assisting a particular person in the commission of a federal crime, Antiterrorism and Effective Death Penalty Act of 1996, Sec. 323; or (3) to prepare for or further a civil disorder, 18 U.S.C. Sec. 231(a)(1). See *United States v. Featherston*, 461 F.2d 1119 (5th Cir.), *cert. denied*, 409 U.S. 991 (1972), and *National Mobilization Committee To End the War in Viet Nam v. Foran*, 411 F.2d 934 (7th Cir. 1969).

— **Robert Corn-Revere**

H. New Law Prohibits Public Access to Chemical Worst-Case Scenarios

In August 1999, Congress approved and the president signed a law prohibiting the Environmental Protection Agency from making available to the public information about the accidental or intentional release of hazardous chemicals at as many as 30,000 facilities across the nation. The Chemical Safety Information, Site Security, and Fuels Regulatory Relief Act exempts so-called "worst-case scenario" reports from the federal Freedom of Information Act and erases provisions of the 1990 amendment to the Clean Air Act.

Congress amended the Clean Air Act in 1990 in response to widespread public anxiety about chemical plant safety. That concern was spurred in part by two highly publicized accidents: the 1984 chemical plant accident in Bhopal, India, that killed more than 2,000 people and the release of toxic gas at the Union Carbide plant in Institute, W.Va., a year later. The amendment required thousands of plants manufacturing, storing, or transporting hazardous chemicals to develop risk management plans (RMPs) that would be available to the public.

As the June 21, 1999 deadline for the filing of these reports approached, the EPA had begun preparations to post the reports on the Internet, as provided for in the Electronic Freedom of Information Act. But chemical manufacturers and federal security agencies raised concerns about the possibility of terrorists accessing the information on the Internet. In a matter of a few months, legislation was drafted and passed reversing the provisions of the Clean Air Act and prohibiting the release of important parts of the chemical plant reports.

The material affected is called the "off-site consequence analysis" (OCA) or "worst-case scenario" information. The OCA portion of a risk management plan consists of one or more worst-case or alternative release scenarios and their possible impact on the surrounding community. These reports contain information about 140 different chemicals, plant accident histories, where and how accidental releases could occur, and populations affected. They do not contain security information, storage tank locations, classified information, or clues as to how a release of chemicals could be triggered.

Provisions of the New Law

The Chemical Safety Information, Site Security, and Fuels Regulatory Relief Act reverses provisions of Section 112(r) of the Clean Air Act; exempts off-site consequence analyses from the federal Freedom of Information Act; overrides provisions of the federal Electronic Freedom of Information Act in the reporting of such information; and preempts state freedom-of-information laws.

The new law limits for at least one year disclosure of the OCA reports to the public as well as any ranking of chemical plants based on the analyses. It also removes from coverage by the RMP program flammable fuels used as fuel or held for sale as fuel at a retail facility. The OCA data will be available to some federal, state, and local officials, as well as to qualified researchers. Any official or researcher making the data available to ordinary citizens faces fines of up to $1 million. Companies that release OCA information on their own must report the release to the EPA, which will maintain a list of those facilities.

By Aug. 5, 2000, federal agencies must publish regulations on public access to OCA data. The FOIA exemption expires only if the government does not issue regulations by the August deadline. The law also requires the federal government to provide reports to Congress on the risks of posting OCA on the Internet as well as the benefits to the public of providing access to that data. Agencies must evaluate how effective the RMP regulations are in reducing the possibility of releases caused by criminal activity; determine how vulnerable chemical facilities are to criminals and terrorists; and outline safety procedures for the transportation of material listed in Section 112(r) of the Clean Air Act. The law also requires the Department of Justice to conduct a study of site security at chemical facilities and to recommend regulations that might reduce vulnerabilities to criminal or terrorist activities.

Although there apparently has been no legal determination as yet, states that require OCA-type reporting themselves may be exempt from restrictions in the federal law.

Impact of the Law

An estimated 40 million Americans live in proximity to the nation's 30,000 chemical facilities. According to the U.S. Chemical Safety Board, each year between 1987 and 1996 there were about 60,000 chemical incidents involving 417 evacuations. There were about 250 deaths and 2,250 injuries each year as a result of these incidents.

Ordinary Americans, activist groups, and local officials have a vital interest in detailed and accurate information about the hazardous and toxic chemicals manufactured and stored at these facilities; plans for reducing impending threats to health and safety; and the impact on the community in the event of an accidental or intentional release of chemicals.

These were among the concerns about the new law raised by access and right-to-know advocates when the Clinton Administration and members of Congress proposed legislation to halt the release of worst-case scenario information. Proponents of the legislation cited the possibility of terrorists obtaining the information if it were put on the Internet.

During testimony before Congress, opponents of the legislation pointed out that of the hundreds of thousands of reported releases of chemicals at U.S. facilities, not a single one was the result of criminal or terrorist sabotage. They also pointed out that denying citizen access to this information on the Internet did not reduce inherent hazards or physically "harden" a site against accidents or criminal activity. They also cited the need for a national database providing comprehensive information about the size and nature of the potential for chemical releases.

Such an official resource would provide authoritative data for accurate and timely information during emergencies; a way for families and firms moving to new communities to assess the risks; and an instrument for journalists and researchers to measure the performance of elected officials, government agencies, and chemical manufacturers in improving safety and security. For example, OMB Watch and the Unison Institute have posted a searchable database of 14,000 RMP reports, some of which contain OCA information, on the Right To Know Network's Web site. Print and broadcast reports utilizing that information have alerted a number of communities to chemical dangers.

Interestingly, many of the same arguments for prohibiting public access to worst-case scenario databases were made against the Toxic Release Inventory program when it was proposed several years ago. But since it was implemented by the EPA, the annual report has led to significant reductions in chemical releases as well as improved safety and security in communities across the nation.

— **Paul K. McMasters**

B-   B-

I. Key Question in Digital Defamation Suits: Who Has Jurisdiction in a Virtual World?

Libel suits based on Internet postings once seemed destined to dominate the field. The volume of such litigation has subsided quite markedly in the last year or two, and probably for several distinct reasons. Most important was the inclusion by Congress in the Communications Decency Act of a provision (Section 230) that immunizes Internet service providers from liability based on material posted by any other speaker or writer.

The U.S. Court of Appeals for the Fourth Circuit, in *Zeran v. America Online*, 129 F.3d 327 (4th Cir. 1997), gave an early and broadly protective interpretation to that law, even where the victim of libelous postings had unsuccessfully asked the ISP to remove the offending material. Since that ruling, libel plaintiffs seem to have assumed that Internet service providers are no longer among possible defendants.

That view was buttressed by a federal district judge's ruling in the libel suit brought by Sidney and Jacqueline Blumenthal against Matt Drudge and America Online over a clearly erroneous and damaging accusation contained in an early issue of the online *Drudge Report*. Even though AOL had proclaimed, only weeks earlier, its mutually beneficial engagement of Drudge and his Internet gossip column, Judge Paul Friedman dismissed all claims against the ISP under Section 230 — leaving potential recourse for libel only against an employee or a direct action of the provider.

The Blumenthal/Drudge case continues its tortuous course through Judge Friedman's court — mired in contentious discovery pleadings that provoked the judge to write in the spring of 1999 that attorneys on both sides were "acting like children" and exhibited behavior "that gives the legal profession a bad name." Important substantive issues of digital defamation law are unlikely to be resolved for quite some time.

A Question of Jurisdiction

Meanwhile, the Blumenthal/Drudge case involves another issue that has recently been before a number of other courts — that of jurisdiction over a nonresident libel defendant. In Matt

Drudge's case jurisdiction in the District of Columbia courts seemed almost easy; though he had moved to California, many of his subscribers and most of his sources (with whom he had frequent e-mail contact) were in the District, where the suit was filed, and the major focus of his gossip items was the environs of the Nation's Capital. Thus it seemed proper to Judge Friedman to retain the suit against Drudge while dismissing AOL as a defendant.

The jurisdictional issue has, however, been more complex in other recent cases. The simple rule emerging through myriad cases is that mere availability in the forum state of access to a passive Web site, with consequent harm to the reputation of a resident of that state, is insufficient to confer jurisdiction — at least under the "long arm" statutes of most states, if not under the Due Process Clause as well. There must be something more, often termed "posting plus." Where a defendant actively conducts business in the forum state, even if only through the Web site, that will suffice for jurisdiction.

Thus early in 1999 one federal court found jurisdiction on the basis of "entering into contracts with residents ... that involve knowing and repeated transmission of computer files over the Internet." *Millennium Enterprises, Inc. v. Millennium Music LP*, 33 F. Supp. 2d 907 (D. Ore. 1999). Other types of interactivity — especially for commercial purposes — are also likely to support jurisdiction over an out-of-state Web site and its operator.

Apart from sustained interactivity, there may be other persuasive factors. In another very recent case, a federal court found jurisdiction because of locally oriented and targeted subject matter — specifically, the then-imminent visit of the Pope to St. Louis — as the focus of the lawsuit. The court found sufficient evidence that the California Web site operator "intended to reach Internet users in Missouri" and was therefore amenable to suit in its courts, at least with respect to the targeted messages, without interactivity. *Archdiocese of St. Louis v. Internet Entertainment Group, Inc.*, 34 F. Supp. 2d 1145 (E.D. Mo. 1999).

Finally, there has been recent debate over the significance of an electronic relationship with entities that happen to be located in the forum state. In a celebrated libel case *Jewish Defense Organization, Inc. v. Superior Court*, 72 Cal. App. 4th 1045 (Cal. App. 1999), the state appeals court declined to assert jurisdiction over a nonresident Web site operator for an alleged libel of a California resident. After several non-Internet contacts proved insufficient, the court assessed the legal import of contracts the defendant had entered with California-based Internet service providers to operate its Web site, and ruled that such contracts were also inadequate as a basis for jurisdiction.

Though the defendant was well aware of the location of the ISPs, and had e-mail communication with them from New York, such a relationship was "insufficient to constitute purposeful availment and does not satisfy the due process requirements for specific jurisdiction." Mere foreseeability that injury might befall a California resident's reputation would not, by itself, suffice.

The Old Dominion: New Jurisdictional Hotspot

Such issues are bound to be more contentious in Virginia because of the physical presence there of the nation's dominant provider, America Online, Inc. There is already a clear split between federal and state courts on that precise issue. In *Bochan v. La Fontaine*, 1999 U.S. Dist. LEXIS 8253 (E.D. Va. 1999), federal district Judge T.S. Ellis, III probed the status of two non-Virginia libel defendants for posting on Internet newsgroups statements that were extremely damaging to the plaintiff. One defendant was clearly subject to Virginia's courts on the basis of substantial business activity in the Commonwealth.

The other defendant, however, had no such contacts; jurisdiction in his case could rest only on his use of an AOL account as the pathway to the newsgroup on which he posted the offending statements about the plaintiff. Ruling as a matter of first impression, Judge Ellis found the use of a Virginia-based ISP sufficient to support jurisdiction, at least under a long-arm law that approaches the limits of what due process permits. Since the essential act of publication was effected by and through an AOL USENET server physically located in the Old Dominion, "there is a sufficient act in Virginia" to satisfy the jurisdictional standard.

A month later a state judge reached a different conclusion in a factually different but legally analogous case. Pennsylvania state judge Joan Orrie Melvin had been the target of a highly damaging accusation posted early in 1999 on an anonymous political gossip Web site. Since the Web site had been posted through America Online, Judge Melvin brought a libel suit against AOL in a Virginia court, choosing the county in which the server was physically located, and claiming that presence as the basis of jurisdiction. Through the suit she hoped to discover the identity of her nameless accuser.

A somewhat unlikely ally, the Virginia American Civil Liberties Union, came to AOL's aid in seeking dismissal of the case on jurisdictional grounds. (ACLU's executive director expressed his fear that otherwise Virginia courts would be flooded with remote cases; "someone in China [would] be able to sue a South African in Loudoun County ... based on something said on the Internet.") In late June, a state judge agreed and dismissed the suit. *Melvin v. Doe*, No. 21942 (Va. Cir. Ct., Loudoun County, June 24, 1999). Though the nameless Web gossip columnist actually made a special appearance, the judge found that the use of a local server to post material by someone having no other Virginia contacts fell short of the "minimum contacts" which both state law and the federal Constitution required.

Given this divergence, it is not easy to predict the future significance of an ISP's physical presence in determining jurisdiction. Where other contacts exist — interactivity, targeting local events or people, or doing business in the forum state by conventional means — there should be little doubt about jurisdiction. But where the use of a local server provides the only possible rationale, the courts of those states in which such entities make their homes will need to assess not only technical issues under state long-arm laws, but also the larger policy implications of grounding jurisdiction on physical locations that have little meaning in a virtual world.

— **Robert M. O'Neil**

J. Online Versions of School Publications and Students' Personal Web Sites Pose Thorny Issues for Courts

Issues surrounding the constitutional rights of high school students are not new to the courts. From *West Virginia Board of Education v. Barnette*, 319 U.S. 624 (1943), to *Vernonia School District v. Acton*, 515 U.S. 646 (1995), courts have struggled to balance the need to protect minors' civil liberties with school administrators' need to maintain order and discipline in their schools.

In the First Amendment arena, *Tinker v. Des Moines School District*, 393 U.S. 503 (1969), and *Hazelwood School District v. Kuhlmeier*, 484 U.S. 260 (1988), established that students do not shed their constitutional rights when attending public school, but that administrators can promulgate guidelines that have the effect of limiting speech and press rights if they advance the educational mission of the institution. These cases gave administrators the right to censor school-sponsored media that may disrupt the school environment, while leaving relatively unmolested students' right to engage in nondisruptive expression at school and fully protected expression outside the school.

Despite the guidelines in these decisions, there continues to be a tension between students who wish to criticize school policies and administrators concerned with maintaining a secure and orderly learning environment. This tension has manifested itself in scholastic journalism as students begin to put their publications on the Internet, and has also spilled outside the schoolhouse gate as students set up their own Web sites using family computers.

This online environment has created a new First Amendment battleground where students' rights are threatened by school administrators responding to calls for safer schools after the panic caused by the Columbine massacre. As students turn to the Internet to express their opinions on issues ranging from school violence to school fashions, administrators watch warily, ready to challenge and punish anything considered inappropriate or dangerous.

School-Sponsored Publications

In *Hazelwood*, the Supreme Court granted school authorities the power to control the content of student publications to the extent the administration has legitimate reasons and a "valid educational purpose." Legitimate justifications include libel, privacy, copyright, and safety concerns. Administrators cannot, however, exercise viewpoint discrimination or censor controversial pieces that are not a threat to the school environment. In reality, however, many student publications are sanitized by principals seeking to protect a school's image.

On its face, *Hazelwood* is confined to physical publications sponsored by the school. However, the reasoning in the decision has been expanded to the Internet. Administrators are seeking to exert the same influence over online versions of student publications as well as materials designed specifically for the World Wide Web.

Most often, school authorities fear the Web will attract harmful elements to the school in ways not possible with more conventional media. Although there has been no litigation on the subject, some schools have begun to take precautions against perceived threats from the Web. For example, at Maize High School in Kansas, the journalism class decided to create an online edition of the school newspaper. The administration allowed the site on the condition that the last names of students appearing in the paper be omitted. See Lisa Napoli, "Schools' online publications face curbs of their own," *New York Times*, May 7, 1999. The school district stated that making the full names of students available online was dangerous, as anyone in the world could have access to the site.

Some districts set different standards for online editions, basing their decision on the Federal Education Records Privacy Act of 1974. The Act prevents schools from releasing certain confidential information about particular students without their permission. At Palmetto High School in Miami, the school's online edition of *The Panther* continues to run photographs of students with their full names, in direct opposition to school guidelines that prohibit the use of photographs or names of students. See Jodi Matthews, "Online student publications held to higher standard than print counterparts," *free! The Freedom Forum Online*, May 13, 1999 <www.freedomforum.org/press/1999/5/13schoolsites.asp>. Because safety is seen as a legitimate educational purpose — especially after the recent violent incidents in several schools — the limitations placed upon official school publications appearing on the Internet seem likely to be upheld by the courts.

Off-Campus Publications

More often in the news and the courts are cases in which students have been punished for creating a personal Web site at home on their own time, which was critical of either the school or a specific school employee. Students have been suspended or expelled, and cases have been filed or threatened, in South Carolina, Wisconsin, Pennsylvania (twice), Ohio (twice), Georgia, Washington, Indiana, and Texas.

The most prominent of these incidents was litigated in a Missouri federal court in *Beussink v. Woodland R-IV School District*, 30 F. Supp. 1175 (E.D. Mo. 1998). Brandon Beussink, a student at Woodland High School, used his home computer to create a Web site critical of the school, its teachers, and the principal. He also created a hyperlink to the school's home page and invited others to voice their criticisms. This commentary used vulgar and profane language. When Principal Yancy Poorman learned of the Web site he suspended Beussink for 10 days, causing Beussink to fail each of his classes because of the district's absenteeism policy. Additionally, he ordered Beussink to "clean up his home page or clear it out."

In an effort to avoid failing high school for exercising his First Amendment rights, Beussink, with his parents, filed suit against the district seeking to enjoin the school from failing him. Judge Rodney Sippel granted the injunction, holding that a student's off-campus speech or other expression that causes no disturbance on campus cannot be proscribed by school authorities. Judge Sippel found that Poorman's suspension of Beussink was illegitimate because Poorman did not, reasonably or otherwise, believe the speech would interfere with school discipline nor did the page cause a disturbance on campus. Instead, the principal was "upset by the content of the home page." The court found that "disliking or being upset by the content of a student's speech is not an acceptable justification for limiting student speech under *Tinker.*"

While the *Beussink* court gave great weight to the fact that the home page had not caused any disturbance on campus, the Student Press Law Center indicates that off-campus publications, including Web sites, are immune from the authority of school officials. Some courts, however, have allowed districts to punish students for off-campus speech. See *The Other Side of the Schoolhouse Gate*, Student Press Law Center Report, Fall 1997 <www.splc.org/report/f97report/f97p20.html>.

In the past, cases have involved underground newspapers produced off-campus. When districts tried to punish this out-of-school speech, courts sided with students and protected their speech rights. The SPLC Report cites *Sullivan v. Houston Independent School District*, 307 F. Supp. 1328 (S.D. Tex. 1969), to support this proposition. Specifically, the *Sullivan* court held that "school officials may not judge a student's behavior while he is in his home with his family." Furthermore, the court in *Thomas v. Granville Central School District*, 607 F.2d 1043 (2d Cir. 1979), found that even when students make occasional use of school property to create the speech, in this case school typewriters, school administrators do not have the right to regulate students' after-school activities.

While principals and others have the power to control and edit school-sponsored Internet activities, they have no authority to control or punish students who speak and write on their own time, from their own computers, even when the school is criticized in a vulgar and profane manner. See SPLC Report, Fall 1997. School officials have had a difficult time understanding the scope of their authority in these matters, but the courts have supported students' rights by enjoining punishments and allowing the reposting of legal material. This support in the few litigated cases has prompted other schools in the same situation to rescind punishments and settle cases out of court. Though it is likely that students will continue to be drawn into these free speech battles, the law appears to be on their side.

— Margaret A. Gorzkowski

K. Global Bookseller Amazon.com Grapples With Foreign Courts on Internet Libel, Prior Restraint

Most media lawyers are, by now, familiar with the chilling effect of libel laws outside the United States. The bar often has succeeded in persuading U.S. courts not to enforce judgments against U.S. defendants based on the laws of the United Kingdom, India, and other countries because those countries' laws do not have protections parallel to those contained in the First Amendment. In cases such as *Matusevich v. Telnikoff*, a 1998 decision of the U.S. Court of Appeals for the District of Columbia Circuit, courts have held that it would offend the First Amendment for U.S. courts to recognize a British libel judgment based on speech that would have been protected under U.S. law. *Matusevich v. Telnikoff*, 877 F. Supp. 1 (D.D.C. 1995), *answering question certified from U.S. Court of Appeals*, 347 Md. 561, 702 A.2d 230 (1997), *conforming to judgment of Maryland Court of Appeals*, 1998 U.S. App. LEXIS 556 (D.C. Cir. May 5, 1998).

For a media distributor operating across international boundaries on the Internet, however, the legal rules governing foreign liability are not clearly defined. Relying on U.S. courts not to enforce foreign judgments may not be sufficient to protect against the risks of potential defamation actions. U.S. content and e-commerce Web sites may well be doing business in the foreign countries that enter judgments against them, and thus must be concerned with the impact of those rulings on the content they can publish and the items they can sell. As a result, foreign law may chill U.S. speech, as Internet bookseller Amazon.com discovered in 1999.

Amazon is a Seattle-based Web site that takes orders for books, videos, games, music, and other goods over the Internet. Since it was founded in 1995, the site claims to have served more than 10 million customers in 160 countries. Its rich catalogue of available works makes it a godsend in countries where diverse bookstores do not exist, and its discounts and broad availability make it popular even where bricks-and-mortar bookstores are plentiful. Amazon has become the leading electronic commerce site on the Internet, with an astronomical market capitalization to match. This combination of spectacular valuation and international reach, of course, makes the bookseller a prime target for litigation — particularly by those bent on suppressing controversial opinions.

A Piece of Blue Sky

Scientology and the Northern Irish conflict have brought Amazon squarely into the spotlight. The first dispute concerned the book *A Piece of Blue Sky* by British writer Jon Atack, which contained a critical examination of Scientology and its founder, L. Ron Hubbard. Courts in the United Kingdom had ruled in a 1995 case that the book defamed Hubbard under UK law and had issued an injunction against its distribution.

Amazon discovered in February 1999 that the book was subject to an injunction barring sale and removed it from distribution. Unfortunately, Amazon's action meant that the book — also distributed internationally online on the Web sites of Barnes & Noble and Borders Books — would be unavailable to Amazon customers in any of the countries served by Amazon.com.

Following Amazon's action, an article on popular Internet news source Wired News provoked a blistering round of cyber-criticism against Amazon. Postings to Internet newsgroups, particularly those concerning the controversial Scientology movement, criticized Amazon for pulling the book from its Web site. Amazon's actions, many asserted, had the effect of extending the UK injunction to numerous countries where it had no effect — including the United States. (The Scientology movement has been active both in libel and copyright litigation and has succeeded in asserting copyright to its basic texts, thus preventing them from being broadly distributed.) After 24 hours, Amazon reversed course and said it would return the book to its list of offerings on its main Web site. It did not, however, return the book to its UK Web site.

The Committee: Political Assassination in Northern Ireland

This was, however, only the beginning of Amazon's legal travails. In late May 1999, David Trimble, a Northern Irish activist, sued Amazon for libel based on its distribution of *The Committee: Political Assassination in Northern Ireland*, a work by Irish investigative journalist Sean McPhilemy. The suit was timed to coincide with the paperback release of the book, which has gained attention worldwide. Trimble also sued the author and the publisher, Roberts Rinehart Publishers.

The book is also subject to litigation in the United States by plaintiffs David and Albert Prentice. The pair filed a $100-million libel case in the District of Columbia Superior Court. *Prentice v. McPhilemy*, Civ. Action No. 4309-98 (filed June 22, 1998). The plaintiffs found that United States courts were not as willing to restrain publication as foreign courts may be. In May 1999, in fact, Judge Noel Kramer denied the plaintiffs' discovery requests attempting to obtain the author's notes.

In denying the discovery request, the court ruled that "the public's interest in the receipt of news and information" outweighed the plaintiffs' interest in obtaining discovery of the author's notes. In the first decision to interpret the District of Columbia's 1992 shield law, the court found that the law does apply to libel defendants. It also noted that the plaintiffs chose to file suit in a jurisdiction in which a shield law would apply. The court refused to find any exceptions in the shield law for information gathered by nonresident journalists or information collected overseas, finding that "to impose such limitations would not further the primary purpose of the Act, namely, to encourage the free flow of information to residents of the District."

At the time of the suit, the book was published only in the United States. But because of Internet sales, largely through Amazon, its publisher asserts that *The Committee* was rated as one of the top-selling books in the United Kingdom. In the case of *The Committee*, the publishers saw the combination of American publishing and Internet distribution as a way to reach an international audience that otherwise could not be reached. As the publisher's Web site states, "due to lack of laws protecting freedom of the press and freedom of expression, and official censorship in Britain, as well as libel laws that heavily favor those named in the book, *The Committee* cannot presently be published in Britain or Ireland.... By publishing this book in the United States, we are able to present the evidence of this shocking conspiracy to the world for the first time." The Web site does not, however, sell the book to residents of Ireland or the UK.

Once again, Amazon confronted the question of whether it should continue to sell a controversial book. Unlike the Scientology instance, however, the decision implied different consequences because Amazon itself was a libel defendant. In June 1999 the company made a split decision. It withdrew *The Committee* from its UK site, Amazon.co.uk. It continues, however, to sell the book through its U.S. Web site, Amazon.com. Amazon.co.uk does not provide a direct link from its British Web site to the American site where the book still can be purchased, but some sources speculated that British residents still could purchase the book through the U.S. Web site. (Whether a purchase from a U.S. Web site with delivery into the UK would be different as a matter of law from a purchase from a UK Web site is quite unclear.) This decision has not satisfied the plaintiff. Jason McCue, the plaintiff's lawyer, was quoted on BBC as threatening legal action against Amazon.com in the United States if it fails to withdraw the book in the United States as well.

It is hardly surprising that plaintiffs would choose the United Kingdom as a libel forum. UK law requires the defendant to prove the truth of allegedly defamatory statements. The plaintiff need not prove anything like our U.S. standard of "actual malice," regardless of whether the plaintiff is a public figure or public official. Rather, malice is presumed from the mere act of publishing. Libel in the UK is, essentially, a strict liability offense.

The conflict illustrates the extent to which the Internet promises to strengthen freedom of expression by making one country's restrictions on speech more porous. By marketing internationally, Amazon extends the reach of authors to a worldwide audience even if local governments might object to their ideas. But this conflict illustrates equally the potential for domestic courts to chill expression in countries beyond their reach. Whether the chill prevails will depend upon the resolve of the bookseller and its ability to defend itself against legal actions filed in unfriendly forum states.

— **Kurt Wimmer**

L. Federal Election Commission Opens Inquiry About Regulating Online Political Speech

In 1999 the Federal Election Commission (FEC) launched an inquiry to examine the application of federal election law to political activity on the Internet. The Commission noted that there has been a dramatic increase in the use of the Internet to conduct campaign activity in recent years, which raises a number of issues regarding the applicability of the Federal Election Campaign Act of 1971 (FECA). Federal Election Commission, *Notice of Inquiry: Use of the Internet for Campaign Activity*, Notice 1999-24. The FEC solicited comments on the implications of applying federal election law to Internet speech to help the Commission decide whether to issue a notice of proposed rulemaking.

Much of the inquiry is directed at the contribution and expenditure limits of FECA, which the Commission noted "are at least facially applicable to a wide range of activity, including some activity that could be conducted on the Internet." Although it sought comment on the application of such regulations, the FEC also asked commenters to address the threshold question of "whether campaign activity conducted on the Internet should be subject to the Act and the Commission's regulations at all." In particular, it encouraged commenters to discuss aspects of the Commission's current regulations that may affect or inhibit the use of the Internet in ways that may not have been anticipated or intended when the regulations were promulgated, and which may now be inappropriate when applied to Internet activity."

FECA requires candidates, political parties, and PACs to file disclosure reports regarding their election-related activity, and also imposes restrictions and limitations on the amounts that may be contributed to candidates, parties, and PACs by individuals, corporations, labor organizations, and other committees. Recent experience has shown that such campaign regulations may impinge on the political speech of corporations, news organizations, and individuals on the Internet.

Free Sites for Candidates Quashed

In 1996 CompuServe tried its hand at campaign reform by emulating the actions of various broadcast networks that had offered free time to political candidates during the presidential campaign. In particular, CompuServe proposed to provide free member accounts to federal candidates on a nonpartisan basis to permit them to post position papers and to facilitate e-mail communication with voters. CompuServe already provided similar free accounts to many journalists, schools, charities, and nonprofit organizations.

Despite that fact, the Commission ruled that providing such accounts to candidates would constitute a prohibited corporate contribution unless CompuServe could show that it provided the accounts to nonpolitical customers in the ordinary course of business and on the same terms and conditions, *i.e.*, the "usual and normal charge." FEC Advisory Opinion 1996-2. The Commission also said that even if the corporation could show that it provided free accounts in the ordinary course of business, the promotional value derived by the vendor in the form of prestige, goodwill, and increased usage by other members did not constitute adequate consideration to satisfy the "usual and normal charge" requirement. The ruling led CompuServe to abandon the plan.

Under FECA, and as the First Amendment requires, news stories, commentaries, and editorials distributed by a broadcast station, newspaper, or other periodical are exempt from the law (unless the publisher or broadcaster is owned or controlled by a candidate, party, or political committee). But the ability of individuals to be Internet publishers blurs the line between traditional publishers and individual pamphleteers. Judge Lowell Reed of the U.S. District Court for the Eastern District of Pennsylvania wrote in a recent case that in the medium of cyberspace "anyone can build a soap box out of web pages and speak her mind in the virtual village green to an audience larger and more diverse than any the Framers could have imagined. In many respects, unconventional messages compete equally with the speech of mainstream speakers in the marketplace of ideas that is the Internet, certainly more than in most other media." *ACLU v. Reno*, 31 F. Supp. 2d 473, 476 (E.D. Pa. 1999). Accordingly, in its notice of inquiry, the FEC asked how the news story exemption should be applied to the Internet.

Free Speech or Campaign Activity?

The answer to that question may have a significant effect on political publishing on the Internet by individuals since the FEC currently regulates such publications as campaign activity. For example, in 1998 Leo Smith created a Web page to protest efforts to impeach President Clinton. Among other things, Smith's Web site advocated the defeat of Rep. Nancy L. Johnson (R) of Connecticut's Sixth Congressional District, and urged voters to elect her Democratic rival. In an advisory opinion, the FEC ruled that the express advocacy contained on the site triggered FECA requirements that Smith fully identify himself on the Web site and state whether or not the expression was authorized by any candidate.

Without any serious discussion, the Commission brushed aside a recent Supreme Court ruling that individuals have a First Amendment right to engage in anonymous political speech. In addition, the FEC ruled that, assuming his activity was independent of a campaign, Smith would have to file reports with the federal government if his expenditures on the Web site exceeded $250 in a one-year period. FEC Advisory Opinion 1998-22. In short, the reward for political involvement on the Internet is to be ensnared in federal rules that all but require a person to hire a lawyer and an accountant.

Across the political divide, another individual Web site is the subject of an FEC complaint from the George W. Bush campaign. Zack Exley posted what has become an Internet art form — the parody Web site. Exley registered the domain name "www.gwbush.com" and posted a quasi-official looking campaign site that the real Bush operation told the FEC "is filled with libelous and untrue statements whose aim is to damage Governor Bush," including the headline "Just Say 'No' to a Former Cocaine User for President." The Bush campaign has asked the FEC to rule that Exley has violated campaign laws by posting the unflattering Web site.

The FEC's inquiry is expected to address many of the difficult questions raised by the intersection of Internet speech and federal regulation of political activity. A ruling is anticipated during the 2000 presidential campaign.

— **Robert Corn-Revere**

M. Three Controversial Web Sites Targeted for Shutdown on Different Grounds

Several recent developments suggest growing legal risks for those who post and maintain Web sites with controversial messages or material. During 1999 efforts were made to shut down Web sites dealing with content as diverse as automotive trade secrets, the daily (and uncensored) activities of several female housemates, and a "virtual" race riot in Times Square.

blueovalnews.com

In the summer of 1999, Robert Lane began using his Web site, blueovalnews.com, as the medium for display of materials (including plans, documents, drawings, and blueprints) that proved highly embarrassing to the Ford Motor Company. Ford went to federal district court, claiming that Lane's postings abridged its copyrights and misused trade secrets.

After granting a temporary injunction, Judge Nancy Edmunds reviewed the case carefully and eventually dismissed all of Ford's claims save those that barred posting of legally protected documents in violation of copyright laws. She ruled that an injunction against continuation of the Web site would amount to a prior restraint in clear violation of the First Amendment.

Judge Edmunds also rejected Ford's claim that Lane's postings should be treated as commercial speech, and therefore less fully protected, because he had once talked of selling some of the blueprints and because the site contained a link bearing the message "advertise on us." Such indicia, ruled Judge Edmunds, provided "no evidence of a specific product offered for sale, and no evidence that Lane's motivation in publishing his Web site was in fact economic." This judgment thus represented a major victory for an outspoken corporate critic as the operator of a less than fully deferential Web site.

voyeurdorm.com

Less clear is the legal status of another novel Web site of 1999, voyeurdorm.com. Its content consists of round-the-clock coverage of several young women who share a house of quite ordinary external appearance in a residential section of Tampa, Fla. The interior of the house is, quite

53

simply, wired with 20 cameras so arranged as to capture — and broadcast over the Internet to those who pay the access fee — the residents' daily activities, clothed and unclad. City officials, upon learning of the Web site, launched several legal challenges.

Most notable, and most likely to yield a novel test case, is Tampa's claim that voyeurdorm.com violates municipal zoning laws that would clearly bar the operation in a residential area of a commercial enterprise that offered intimate views comparable to those that voyeurdorm subscribers may obtain through the Internet. To city officials, the difference in medium does not suspend the zoning system.

For the Web site's operators, however, that difference is crucial. They note the indistinguishable exterior of the house, and the fact that such a "virtual business" entails none of the evils that have justified special zoning of sex shops, adult theaters and bookstores, and other commercial entities. In no sense, they insist, could such inconspicuous use of a house be said to "run down the neighborhood" in ways that have evoked judicial concern and led courts to uphold special "red light" zoning. The Web site's proprietors have promised to take the city to court on such novel First Amendment issues, and the case (like the Web site itself) is certain to be closely watched in the months ahead.

crowdedtheater.com

The third of the year's novel Web sites seems, at least for the moment, to have dodged the bullet. A person known only as Mike Z created a site that he called "crowded theater.com," and on which he posted (as described by a *Village Voice* account) a "Blair Witch style video about a race riot in Times Square."

After concerns had been expressed to law enforcement officials about the site's contents and possible impact, FBI agents visited Z's home, contacted his Internet service provider, and persuaded the ISP to remove the site. The agency, with less than model precision, acknowledged its concern — "not to determine was this something that might generate fear or panic, but was it something that was a record of a plan to carry out a riot."

When word of the site's demise became public, champions of free expression in cyberspace streamed to Z's defense, protesting the action and starting a flaming war against the ISP. Soon crowdedtheater.com reappeared, and soon thereafter an FBI spokesperson announced that any inquiry into Mike Z's Internet postings had been discontinued.

The American Civil Liberties Union, meanwhile, had begun discussions with the owner of the ISP about possible legal remedies he might invoke against the FBI for having threatened punitive action if he failed to remove the suspect Web site. (Under the Communications Decency Act, even without a law enforcement directive an ISP presumably could not be civilly liable to a subscriber for having removed controversial material.) The first battle seems thus to have ended, but may well anticipate future challenges to the content and even the survival of unsettling Internet Web sites.

— Robert M. O'Neil

SECTION II

BROADCASTING AND CABLE TELEVISION

BROADCASTING AND CABLE TELEVISION

The Media Institute and its First Amendment Advisory Council graded the three branches of the federal government and state and local government for their support of the First Amendment regarding the above broadcasting and cable television issues as follows:

Executive Branch	*Legislative Branch*	*Judicial Branch*	*State & Local*
C	B-	C	C

A. Broadband Internet Access Debate Erupts Among Cable Operators, ISPs, Regulators

As cable television systems have begun to offer high-speed Internet connections using cable modems, an intense debate has erupted over proposals to require cable operators to provide access to their broadband platforms by competing Internet Service Providers (ISPs). Labeled "open access" by proponents of such measures, and "forced access" by opponents, the battle has been waged at all three branches of the federal government and at the state and local level as well.

Broadband Internet access allows for substantially greater data speeds than the traditional telephone network, which generally provides speeds of 56 kilobytes per second. In addition to enabling an "always on" connection to the Internet, broadband capability makes possible a wide range of enhanced services including streaming video and telephony services.

By mid-1999, there were 750,000 users of cable broadband Internet services in the United States, and the number of users continued to grow as the technology became more available. Jason L. Riley, "Business world: Faster Web access coming (one day) to a home near you," *Wall Street Journal*, July 14, 1999, at A23. A report issued by the FCC's Cable Services Bureau predicted that there would be 2 million Americans with broadband Internet access by the end of 1999, counting access via cable and other transmission methods, such as digital subscriber line (DSL), and that the number would jump to 78 million by 2008. Cable Services Bureau, *Broadband Today*, Oct. 1999, at 9. About 1 million of those with broadband access in 1999 attained their high-speech connection via cable. *Id.* at 25.

The Access Policy Debate

The merger of AT&T and TCI caused concern among some that AT&T-TCI would have a substantial head start in the provision of high-speed Internet access, and prompted calls for the FCC to impose a broadband access requirement as a condition of approving the merger. The Commission disagreed that access requirements were needed and noted that other competing broadband technologies were evolving. *Applications for Consent to the Transfer of Control of Licenses and Section 214 Authorizations from Tele-Communications, Inc. to AT&T Corp.,* 14

FCC Rcd. 3160, 3207 (1999). The Commission has continued to take the position that broadband deployment is at a nascent stage, and that regulatory intervention at this time would be premature. *Broadband Today,* at 32-33, 41-46.

Far from ending the debate, the FCC's position on broadband access led the interested parties to direct their efforts at other levels of government. Thus, for example, local franchising authorities across the United States examined the AT&T-TCI merger to determine whether local approvals should include access conditions, while other communities considered adopting such requirements as part of their franchising ordinances. Most notably, the City of Portland, Ore., and the County of Multnomah adopted the first mandatory access provision as a result of the AT&T-TCI merger. When AT&T rejected the mandatory access requirement, the franchising authority denied approval for a change of control in TCI's franchises in January 1999.

AT&T challenged the decision in federal court, claiming that the access requirements violated the Cable Act, the Commerce and Contract Clauses of the Constitution, and the First Amendment. In June 1999, the U.S. District Court for the District of Oregon rejected AT&T's claims, and concluded that the city and the county have the power to require access to the cable modem platform as a condition of approving the transfer of TCI's franchises. *AT&T Corp. v. City of Portland*, 43 F. Supp. 2d 1146 (D. Ore. 1999). That decision was appealed to the U.S. Court of Appeals for the Ninth Circuit, and oral argument was heard in November 1999.

As the Portland battle continued, the access war raged on many fronts. Other communities, including Los Angeles, St. Louis, Broward County, Fla., San Francisco, and Fairfax County, Va., among others, considered imposing access requirements, with varying results. Broward County adopted an ordinance requiring broadband access, which was promptly challenged in court. *Comcast Cablevision of Broward County, Inc. v. Broward County*, Case No. 99-6934 (S.D. Fla. 1999). In another action, GTE filed an antitrust claim, alleging that the refusal to provide broadband access on the cable platform was a violation of the Sherman Act. *GTE Internetworking, Inc. v. Tele-Communications, Inc.*, 4 ILR (P & F) 4006 (W.D. Pa. 1999).

A number of states considered legislation to require broadband access, as did federal legislators. Rep. Rick Boucher (D-Va.) introduced the Internet Growth and Development Act of 1999, H.R. 1685, which would require cable networks to provide access to competing ISPs, among a number of other provisions. Similarly, Rep. Bob Goodlatte (R-Va.) introduced the Internet Freedom Act, H.R. 1686, which contained a similar requirement. At the regulatory level, Internet Ventures, Inc. filed a petition for declaratory ruling with the FCC, asking the Commission to require broadband Internet access pursuant to the Cable Act's leased access requirements.

The First Amendment Issue

The many debates over broadband access raise a host of issues involving federal communications and antitrust law, regulatory classification of service, federal preemption of local authority, and questions involving the Contract and Commerce Clauses. For purposes of this Report, however, the relevant disputes center on the First Amendment.

Opponents of broadband access requirements argue that such obligations constitute a form of compelled speech in violation of the principles established in *Miami Herald Publishing Co. v. Tornillo*, 418 U.S. 241 (1974). As such, access requirements should be evaluated under strict scrutiny. Even if evaluated as content-neutral economic regulations akin to must-carry rules, according to this position, access requirements should be struck down because it has not been demonstrated that the need for such measures is real, not conjectural, or that the requirements would alleviate the harm in a direct or material way. *Turner Broadcasting System, Inc. v. FCC*, 512 U.S. 622, 662 (1994). Proponents of access requirements argue that, like must-carry rules, broadband access is content neutral, and that such rules are needed to prevent cable operators from dominating the market for high-speed Internet services, thereby suppressing speech.

The district court in *AT&T Corp. v. City of Portland* rejected AT&T's First Amendment arguments. Noting that AT&T had volunteered to give cable subscribers access to competing ISPs (after obtaining a high-speed connection from the cable operator), the court concluded that an access requirement did not implicate the cable operator's speech interests. 43 F. Supp. 2d at 1154, citing *PruneYard Shopping Center v. Robins*, 447 U.S. 74 (1980). The court concluded that subscribers accessing the Internet via AT&T's cable system would not associate AT&T with the speech offered by competing ISPs. The court ultimately found that the access mandate was an economic regulation subject to intermediate scrutiny, and that the measure was justified by the substantial governmental interest in preserving competition.

The appeal of the district court decision is pending. However, the Ninth Circuit may not reach the First Amendment question. During oral argument, the judges focused significant attention on the proper regulatory classification of cable-based Internet services, an issue that could decide the case on the basis of statutory interpretation.

— **Robert Corn-Revere**

B. FCC Still Grappling With Digital Must-Carry for Cable; Congress Allows Satellites To Deliver Local Signals

The issue of digital must-carry remained unresolved in 1999 as the Federal Communications Commission, broadcasters, and cable operators grappled with the question of which, if any, over-the-air TV signals cable operators should be required to carry while broadcasters convert from analog to digital transmission. Meanwhile, however, direct broadcast satellite (DBS) systems received congressional authorization to begin transmitting the signals of local broadcast stations to their subscribers, subject to must-carry requirements beginning in 2002. (See *The First Amendment and the Media - 1999* for comprehensive background on these topics.)

Must-Carry for Digital Broadcasters

Near the end of 1999, 82 television stations in 36 markets serving over 53 percent of the United States were broadcasting in digital, according to an editorial in *Broadcasting & Cable* magazine. "Fiddling while DTV burns," *Broadcasting & Cable*, Nov. 1, 1999, at 82. On the other hand, this same editorial argues that without more impetus from the FCC, it may be a very long while, if ever, before we reach the required level of digital penetration (85 percent of television households in a market) to trigger broadcasters' return of their current analog spectrum to the FCC.

Decker Anstrom, then president of the National Cable Television Association (NCTA), asserted in late 1998: "The practical reality is that analog spectrum will never be given back in our lifetimes." See Bill McConnell, "Digital must carry: Cable's un-issue," *Broadcasting & Cable*, Dec. 7, 1998, at 12, 13. During the transition period when stations are transmitting both analog and digital signals (presumably with much duplication in programming), the first question is: Which signals will be subject to must-carry?

If and when the transition to digital is completed, the problem arguably becomes even thornier. A digital broadcaster with 6 MHz of spectrum will be able to transmit one high definition channel or several "multiplexed" channels of standard definition, the number depending on the state of compression technology. Which of these will be subject to must-carry? Even on cable systems with large channel capacity, each additional broadcast signal carried may well require the displacement of alternative programming.

The battle lines are being drawn ever more sharply. NCTA's current president, Robert Sachs, flatly states that cable operators will not accept a "double dose" of must-carry. He asserts that additional must-carry requirements are unnecessary, as the major-network stations prefer to negotiate for cable carriage pursuant to retransmission consent rather than invoke statutory rights. See "Sachs seeks to sack must-carry," *Cable TV Law Reporter*, Oct. 27, 1999, at 10. NCTA recently filed a white paper with the FCC setting forth its position and arguing that more marketplace experience is necessary before the FCC makes any decisions on the issue. See "Cable programmers set to storm FCC," *Broadcasting & Cable*, Nov. 1, 1999, at 20.

Not surprisingly, broadcasters take a very different view and dispute cable claims of constrained bandwidth that will produce a channel crunch. See John M. Higgins, "Must-carry: $12B hit or crying wolf?" *Broadcasting & Cable*, April 5, 1999, at 16. Citing a report from the Congressional Budget Office, Paxson Communications Corp. Chairman Lowell W. Paxson argues that, without a strong requirement for cable systems to carry digital signals, "broadcasters will lose the digital marketplace, and the Supreme Court's prediction about the cable bottleneck will come true." Lowell W. Paxson, "Digital must-carry must happen," *Broadcasting & Cable*, Oct. 25, 1999, at 22. Without such must-carry, Paxson claims, "the hundreds of television stations not owned by the four major networks will be left at the mercy of cable." *Id*.

Voluminous papers were filed with the FCC in its pending digital must-carry proceeding, *In the Matter of Carriage of the Transmissions of Digital Television Broadcast Stations*, *Notice of Proposed Rulemaking, CS Docket No. 98-120*, FCC 98-153 (released July 10, 1998). The chief of the FCC's Cable Services Bureau promised to issue a staff report on must-carry by the end of 1999. Whatever its position, this paper is sure to provoke more controversy and, ultimately, litigation.

DBS Carriage of Local Broadcast Signals

The situation regarding must-carry for satellite systems is similar but was significantly advanced by enactment in late 1999 of the Satellite Television Home Viewers Act (STHVA) as part of the omnibus spending bill President Clinton signed on Nov. 29, 1999. Satellite systems, unlike local cable systems, traditionally have been national services and therefore, until recently, have not come under pressure (nor been authorized) to carry local broadcast signals. Now, however, with its market penetration growing rapidly (increasing 42.7 percent in the last year alone), DBS seems to have the potential to develop into a prime competitor to cable. But to compete fully, DBS must be able to offer subscribers access to their local broadcast stations, or "local into local" service.

Advancing technology seems to allow satellite systems the increasing ability to carry a significant number of local broadcast stations along with their current diverse fare. See *In the Matter of Satellite Delivery of Network Signals to Unserved Households for Purposes of the Satellite Home Viewer Act, Notice of Proposed Rulemaking, CS Docket No. 98-201,* FCC 98-302 (released Nov. 17, 1998), para. 43. Still, the satellite services are concerned about being overwhelmed by carriage requirements that are too broad too soon in some markets. But the National Association of Broadcasters and others expressed concerns that satellite systems might choose to carry only some of the most popular broadcast stations to the considerable detriment of those left out. These concerns led to proposals that would require any satellite carrier who wished to offer any local into local service in a particular market to commit to carrying a large number, if not eventually all, of those local stations.

Congress failed to enact appropriate legislation in 1998. Fairly early in 1999, however, the Commerce and Judiciary committees of the House and Senate each reported out a bill. Despite considerable pressure on Congress to act, political squabbling and the need for compromises threatened to defeat the legislative efforts for most of the term. Particularly controversial was a provision for $1.25 billion in federal loan guarantees for satellite and cable companies to subsidize development of rural television service. Agreement on the final measures eventually was reached when this provision was eliminated, together with language that would have prohibited any online service provider from transmitting any part of local broadcasters' signals without their permission.

As enacted, the STHVA grants satellite television providers the authority to immediately begin carrying local TV signals for six months while they work out carriage agreements with local broadcast stations. Local broadcasters won provisions that prohibit satellite services from carrying another network affiliate to households within approximately 75 miles of a local affiliate, about twice the radius by which cable companies are bound. By Jan. 1, 2002, satellite companies must carry all local television signals in any market they choose to serve with local into local service.

The STHVA is clearly a competitive boon both for satellite providers and subscribers who now may have options in addition to cable television service. Still, there may not be enough satellite capacity to serve all satellite subscribers with local broadcast service. And, although satellite providers may be able to charge some subscribers more for local broadcast stations, it may prove very expensive for satellite companies to provide such service in all markets. See Seth Schiesel, "Local signals may be costly for satellite TV providers," *New York Times*, Dec. 13, 1999, at C1.

Much of this will depend on how broad beam and spot beam satellites are deployed and managed to cover the continental United States, and on how the FCC resolves regulatory uncertainties regarding the extent of must-carry obligations as it writes the rules to implement the new act. *Id.* Nonetheless, Congress may have significantly improved the competitive structure of the video marketplace while minimizing legal and constitutional issues.

— Laurence H. Winer

C. Court Criticizes Personal Attack, Political Editorializing Rules but Refuses To Vacate Them

In August 1999, the U.S. Court of Appeals for the District of Columbia Circuit soundly criticized the Federal Communications Commission's personal attack and political editorializing rules, although it ultimately refused to vacate them.[1] *Radio-Television News Directors Association v. FCC*, 184 F.3d 872 (D.C. Cir. 1999). This decision follows the FCC's 18-year consideration and eventual rejection of a petition by the Radio-Television News Directors Association (RTNDA) and National Association of Broadcasters (NAB) to repeal the rules. The net effect of the court's ruling is to keep in place these rules, which are antithetical to First Amendment values, even as the court rejected a variety of theories advanced by the Commission to justify the rules.

Background

The personal attack rule requires that "[w]hen, during the presentation of views on a controversial issue of public importance, an attack is made upon the honesty, character, integrity, or like personal qualities of an identified person or group, the licensee shall" provide the person or group attacked with a tape or transcript and a reasonable opportunity to respond. 47 C.F.R. Sec. 73.1920 (West 1999). The political editorial rule mandates that "[w]here a licensee, in an editorial, [e]ndorses or, [o]pposes a legally qualified candidate or candidates, the licensee shall" provide the other qualified candidates for the same office with notice and an opportunity to respond. *Id.* at Sec. 73.1930. The rules were promulgated to effectuate the FCC's long-standing "Fairness Doctrine," which required broadcasters to present both sides of controversial issues of public importance.

NAB first challenged these rules in 1980 on the grounds that, among other things, they chilled speech and infringed on broadcasters' First Amendment freedoms. RTNDA joined NAB in its challenge in 1983. While this petition was pending, the Commission in 1987 repealed the Fairness Doctrine. Among the many reasons for the FCC's repeal was that the factual predicate for the doctrine — the scarcity of broadcasters — no longer existed. The FCC also found that the doctrine had produced a "chilling effect" on broadcasters' coverage of issues of public importance.

In 1998 the Commission, by an equally divided vote (one of the five commissioners did not participate), refused to repeal the personal attack and political editorializing rules. Even though the Commission had adopted the rules as a means "to effectuate important aspects of the ... Fairness Doctrine," *Amendment of Part 73 of the Rules*, 8 F.C.C.2d 721, 722 (1967), Commissioners Ness and Tristani opined that "these rules are based on the public interest standard, and are not dependent on the continued existence of the fairness doctrine." *Joint Statement of Commissioners Ness and Tristani Concerning the Political Editorial and Personal Attack Rules*, FCC 83-484 (June 22, 1998), at ¶ 54.

Court Appeal

On appeal, NAB and RTNDA argued that the FCC's failure to repeal the rules violated the Administrative Procedures Act as well as the First Amendment. On the First Amendment argument, NAB and RTNDA asserted that, in light of the demise of the Fairness Doctrine, any purported government interest in balance or diversity would not be substantial because the extraordinary variety of the media marketplace more than adequately serves such interests without intrusive government regulation.

Also, NAB and RTNDA showed that the practical effect of the challenged rules is to impede balance and diversity in the presentation of issues of public importance. NAB and RTNDA further maintained that the challenged rules should be subject to strict scrutiny, because the FCC has sent the signal that the scarcity rationale no longer justifies relaxed scrutiny for content-based regulation of broadcaster speech.

The court disagreed with the parties' first argument that the demise of the Fairness Doctrine necessarily required repeal of the challenged rules. It concluded that the challenged rules are narrower and more refined than the Fairness Doctrine. Thus, the court said it was conceivable that the FCC could reasonably conclude that the public interest may not require fairness to all views all of the time, but that fairness to views in certain defined circumstances was nonetheless desirable.

The court, however, did accept the parties' second argument that the practical effect of the challenged rules was to "interfere with the editorial judgment of professional journalists and entangle the government in day-to-day operations of the media." *RTNDA*, 184 F.3d at 881. The court also emphasized that the "challenged rules by their nature ... chill at least some speech, and impose at least some burdens on activities at the heart of the First Amendment." *Id*. at 887. As such, the court stated that the FCC "must explain why the public would benefit from rules that raise these policy and constitutional doubts." *Id*. at 882.

FCC's Justifications Rebuffed

The court then considered and discarded each of the FCC's six justifications for the rules. First, the court agreed that it was "no doubt sound" to suppose that "the public has an interest in hearing both sides of each issue on which a broadcaster elects to focus." *Id*. However, it observed that the FCC did not present "a plausible explanation why political editorials and personal attacks are sufficiently meaningful to warrant regulation when other kinds of topics, editorials, and attacks do not." *Id*.

Second, the court rejected the FCC's misplaced reliance on *Red Lion Broadcasting Co. v. FCC*, 395 U.S. 367 (1969), as "flawed to the extent that it relies on a thirty-year-old conclusion ... to justify the decision not to repeal the [rules] in the face of modern challenges to the rules' consistency with the FCC's regulatory mandate." *RTNDA*, 184 F.3d at 882. Third, the court rejected the FCC's argument that it has the power to regulate broadcast frequencies, stating that "[t]he mere fact that the FCC has the power to regulate broadcasters more intensely than other media does not also mean that it may impose any obligation it sees fit." *Id*. at 883.

Fourth, the court rebuffed the FCC's contention that the statutorily mandated equal time doctrine — which requires a licensee who allows a candidate to use its broadcasting station to allow other candidates for the office the same privilege — compels the rules here, which apply when the licensee itself distributes the proscribed content. *Id*. Fifth, the court held that the mere fact that "vibrant debate was good for democracy" cannot itself "explain why editorials about candidates justify federal intervention when other types of editorials or non-editorial programming does not." *Id*. at 884. Last, the court refused to accept the FCC's "conclusory assertion that the rule is a necessary prerequisite for balanced debate on public issues." *Id*. at 885.

Based on these deficiencies in the FCC's justifications, the court determined that the FCC's explanation was insufficient to permit judicial review. The court explained that "[w]ooden application of principles underlying rhetoric ... would disserve the parties and muddle the First Amendment analysis." *Id*. at 887. Thus, the court remanded the case to the FCC for it to explain its rationale in more detail. Once the FCC has explained its rationale a second time, the court will be able to determine whether the rules satisfy the demands of the First Amendment.

— Daniel E. Troy

---

[1] The author of this section, Daniel E. Troy, presented the oral argument of RTNDA and NAB in this case to the U.S. Court of Appeals for the District of Columbia Circuit. His law firm, Wiley, Rein & Fielding, continues to represent RTNDA and NAB.

C+   B-

D. FCC Relaxes Rules on Local Broadcast Ownership but Action Lags on 1998 Biennial Review

In a long-awaited move, the Federal Communications Commission in August 1999 revised its rules on local broadcast station ownership, making it possible for one entity to own two television stations or combination of TV and radio stations in the same market. The FCC also grandfathered the local marketing agreements (LMAs) it had threatened to eliminate only months earlier. The Commission did not, however, raise the 35-percent national audience cap on TV station ownership, nor did it repeal the newspaper / broadcast cross ownership ban. As 1999 ended, the congressionally mandated 1998 Biennial Review of broadcast ownership rules was far from complete, even as the Commission faced the imminent prospect of undertaking the 2000 review.

Television Duopoly Rule

Changes to the duopoly rule were first contemplated in an FCC Notice of Inquiry issued in 1991. The rule prohibited common ownership, operation, or control of two or more television stations with overlapping Grade B contours, and had been a fixture of broadcast regulation for decades. The Commission said the revised rule reflects "growth in the number and variety of media outlets in local markets, including cable and direct broadcast satellite" and is "intended to strengthen the potential of free over-the-air broadcast services to compete ... in the video marketplace." *In the Matter of Review of the Commission's Regulations Governing Television Broadcasting, MM Docket No. 91-221, and Television Satellite Stations Review of Policy and Rules, MM Docket No. 87-8, Report and Order*, FCC 99-209 (released Aug. 6, 1999).

The revised duopoly rule:

- Permits common ownership of two television stations without regard to contour overlap if the stations are in separate Nielsen Designated Market Areas (DMAs).
- Continues to allow common ownership of two stations in the same DMA if their Grade B contours do not overlap.
- Permits common ownership of two television stations in the same DMA if eight full-power independent television stations (commercial or noncommercial) will remain after the merger,

and if one of the stations is not among the top four in the market based on audience share.

- Allows a waiver to permit common ownership of two television stations in the same market where a current licensee is the "only reasonably available buyer" and the station to be purchased is "failed" or "failing."
- Allows a waiver if applicants can show that the combination will result in the construction of a previously unbuilt station.

Radio / Television Cross Ownership Rule

The revised radio / television cross ownership rule (or "one-to-a-market" rule) now allows the owner of one or two television stations in a market to own the following maximum number of radio stations (any combination of AM or FM) in the same market:

- Six radio stations in markets where at least 20 "independent voices" would remain after the merger. (As an alternative to two television and six radio stations, the Commission would allow one TV and seven radio stations.)
- Four radio stations in markets where at least 10 independent voices would remain.
- One radio station regardless of the number of independent voices.

Independent voices are defined as independently owned commercial and noncommercial television and radio stations, daily newspapers, and cable service in the same market as the television station.

Local Marketing Agreements

A local marketing agreement is an arrangement under which one television station provides operational and marketing support for a financially weaker station in the same market. LMAs have often been regarded as a means of skirting the duopoly rule by allowing one entity to control two TV stations in a market. Under the revised duopoly rule, many LMAs will probably disappear as station groups buy up their LMA stations. However, remaining LMAs will be grandfathered for five years until 2004, provided they were arranged before Nov. 5, 1996. They will be reviewed for possible extension on a case-by-case basis under the 2004 Biennial Review. LMAs not eligible for grandfathering must be terminated by Aug. 6, 2001.

In a separate Report and Order released Aug. 6, 1999, the FCC revised its broadcast and cable/MDS ownership attribution rules, which determine how financial interests in stations are to be counted for purposes of the Commission's ownership rules. The FCC added a new time brokerage rule for LMAs and a new "equity/debt plus" rule, and raised the threshold for passive investments from 10 percent to 20 percent of total assets. *Review of the Commission's Regulations Governing Attribution of Broadcast and Cable/MDS Interests, MM Docket No. 94-150, Review of the Commission's Regulations and Policies Affecting Investment in the Broadcast Industry,*

MM Docket No. 92-51, and Reexamination of the Commission's Cross-Interest Policy, MM Docket No. 87-154, Report and Order, FCC 99-207 (released Aug. 6, 1999).

Biennial Review

The Telecommunications Act of 1996 instructed the FCC to conduct a review of its ownership rules every two years beginning in 1998. Ongoing proceedings, like those for the duopoly and one-to-a-market rules, were deemed part of the 1998 Biennial Review. Two other categories of regulation were targeted for review: (1) rules modified by the 1996 Telecom Act, and (2) rules not modified by the Act. At the end of 1999 no action had been taken on a host of issues under review in both categories, notably the rule that limits TV station ownership to a national "audience reach" of 35 percent of television households, and the newspaper / broadcast cross ownership ban that prohibits common ownership of a daily newspaper and broadcast outlet in the same market.

In the omnibus appropriations bill signed by President Clinton on Nov. 29, 1999, Congress gave the FCC 180 days to conclude the 1998 Biennial Review. Pub. L. No. 106-113, Sec. 5003, 113 Stat. 1501 (1999). During these six months the Commission would be expected to issue a notice of proposed rulemaking for any rule it wished to modify or repeal, and to adopt a final report to Congress on the status of the review. Proceedings not completed by the May 2000 deadline presumably would be carried over to the 2000 Biennial Review.

First Amendment Concerns

The FCC's interest in promoting diversity by manipulating ownership requirements raises significant First Amendment concerns. To impose diversity on the media marketplace of ideas, the government must necessarily suppress the free expression of certain speakers by denying them an opportunity to own additional media outlets of their choosing. Those who own a certain type of outlet or a certain number of outlets become, in effect, a disfavored class of speakers whose further speaking opportunities are proscribed by the FCC.

Historically, the Commission has been able to justify this reduced level of First Amendment protection for broadcasters by invoking the scarcity rationale — the idea that broadcast frequencies are somehow uniquely scarce and thus must be controlled by the government. That rationale has been thoroughly demolished, however, by scholars, economists, jurists, and even the 1980s-era Commission itself.

In his dissent from the Report and Order on local broadcast ownership regulations, Com. Harold Furchtgott-Roth noted this fact and raised the constitutional implications surrounding the scarcity question:

[T]he constitutional status of even these "modified" ownership regulations is open to substantial doubt. If spectrum is no longer scarce, then the justification for the lower standard of review afforded to broadcast regulations fades away.... If strict scrutiny applies here — as it does in the context of the print media, the internet, and cable — the constitutionality of these limits on broadcast speech is highly doubtful. "Dissenting statement of Com. Harold W. Furchtgott-Roth," *Report and Order*, FCC 99-209 (released Aug. 6, 1999), at Sec. II.

Com. Furchtgott-Roth also castigated the Commission for stating in the Report and Order that it wished to "encourage" broadcasters to boost media ownership among women and minorities: "If the Commission is not yet willing to make the case for race- and gender-based preferences (I am not sure it ever can), it should not ask broadcasters to do 'voluntarily' what would be well unconstitutional for the Commission to require." *Id.* at Sec. III.

Legislative Action

On Oct. 21, 1999, Sens. John McCain (R-Ariz.) and Conrad Burns (R-Mont.) introduced S. 1766, the Telecommunications Ownership Diversification Act of 1999. The bill would allow owners of telecommunications firms to defer taxes on capital gains if they sell their businesses to "historically disadvantaged individuals," and would provide other incentives "to promote diversity of ownership in telecommunications businesses." The bill was referred to the Senate Finance Committee but no further action has occurred.

A similar bill in the House, the Free Television Viability Act of 1999 (H.R. 3431), was introduced on Nov. 17. It was sponsored by Reps. Eliot L. Engel (D-N.Y.), Sheila Jackson Lee (D-Texas), and Bobby L. Rush (D-Ill.). The measure was referred to the House Commerce Committee and then to the Telecommunications Subcommittee but has languished there.

— Richard T. Kaplar

E. FCC Rulemaking on Low Power Radio Envisions Three Classes of Service

The Federal Communications Commission has decided to create a low power FM radio service in the hope that it will increase diversity in broadcasting while also providing more coverage of interest to local communities. On Feb. 3, 1999, the Commission released a *Notice of Proposed Rulemaking in the Matter of Creation of a Low Power FM Radio Service*, 14 FCC Rcd. 2471 (1999) ("NPRM"). After a long comment process, a Report and Order was released on Jan. 27, 2000. The Commission approved the low power FM service as it was envisioned in the NPRM, with some variations.

In the NPRM, the FCC stated its belief that a low power radio service would provide a low-cost means of serving both urban and rural populations. It specifically identified three goals it hopes to accomplish through the creation of this service: (1) addressing unmet needs for community-oriented radio broadcasting; (2) fostering opportunities for new radio broadcast ownership; and (3) promoting additional diversity in radio voices and program services.

Background

This proceeding is borne of two petitions for rulemaking requesting that the Commission look into the feasibility of creating some form of low power radio service (the NPRM also noted the Commission had received over 13,000 requests in 1998 alone from individuals and groups showing an interest in starting a low power station). The first is known as the "Skinner Petition." It requested three classes of low power FM radio service: a primary class with 50 to 3,000 watts of power that would have a coverage area of approximately 15 miles; a second class with a maximum power of 50 watts and a coverage area of approximately five miles; and a third class consisting of a special event service allowing up to 20 watts of power for 10 days at a time.

The second petition is known as the "Leggett Petition." It proposed a "microradio" service limited to one watt of power and a maximum antenna height of 50 feet. Such stations would broadcast using a cellular arrangement on a single AM and a single FM frequency for all stations nationwide.

These proposals were generally supported through comments filed by small businesses, community groups, hundreds of individual citizens, and small and noncommercial broadcasters. Though they did not agree on the parameters of the proposed service, these commenters were united in their belief that broadcasting has become expensive and that, as a result, the public is being deprived of diverse local voices.

The petitions were opposed by National Public Radio, individual licensees, and various radio broadcasting organizations including the National Association of Broadcasters. These groups claimed that a myriad of stations are already serving local community needs, and maintained that diversity issues should be addressed through changes in ownership rules.

The Commission decided the demands raised by the two petitions for rulemaking and the supporting commenters would best be met by creating more than one type of station. Part of the reason it tentatively settled on a multi-tiered system of low power FM stations was the inherent difficulty of choosing between a higher class-higher power station that would attract significant listeners and a lower class-power station that would appeal to local "niche" programmers offering important community event coverage.

The Commission's first concern was spectrum allocation. It did not intend to create a service beyond any spectrum currently allocated for FM use. At the same time, it did not appear possible to designate one frequency or several frequencies for use by low power FM stations on a nationwide basis.

Three-Tiered System

The NPRM proposed a scheme of operation throughout the FM band in a manner that would cause the least interference to existing services in each community. Three classes of stations were proposed. The first would be known as "LP1000." These stations would operate at a maximum effective radiated power of 1,000 watts, with a maximum antenna height of 60 meters. LP1000 stations using the same frequency would be separated by at least 40 miles, allowing a relatively interference-free signal of about 8.8 miles in each direction. It would be considered a "primary" broadcast service, requiring these stations to protect against interference to all other primary stations while ensuring that they do not receive interference from other primary stations.

The second class of stations would be known as "LP100." These stations would be intended to meet the demand of people wishing to broadcast affordably to communities of moderate size. As the name would indicate, they would have a maximum power of 100 watts with a maximum antenna height of 30 meters, producing a quality signal with an approximate radius of 3.5 miles. LP100 stations would be considered a "secondary" service, meaning they could not cause interference within the protected service contours of existing and future primary stations, nor would they be protected from interference from these stations.

The final class of low power FM station would be known as "microradio." Microradio stations would operate with a maximum antenna height of 30 meters and a maximum power of 10 watts. The coverage area of a given microradio station would be approximately two miles in any direction. These stations would provide very limited coverage of highly local events; the Commission envisioned most of the licensees would be schools, neighborhood groups, and town centers. Although the facilities would be rather small and unsophisticated, the Commission stated it would impose an FCC transmitter certification requirement, noting that uncertified equipment had, in the past, caused dangerous interference to aviation frequencies.

Ownership Issues

The NPRM next addressed a series of ownership issues, including local and cross ownership, national ownership caps, and residency requirements. This is one of the key issues the Commission will consider, as it views low power radio as the primary vehicle for enhancing diversity, increasing new program services, and providing opportunities to new broadcasters. These goals might be difficult to meet if low power FM stations are offered to existing broadcasters or if a number of new low power FM facilities in an area are under common control.

The Commission tentatively concluded strict local and cross ownership restrictions would be appropriate for the low power FM service. No person with an attributable interest in a full broadcast station would be allowed to have any ownership in a low power FM or microradio station in any market. Joint sales agreements, time brokerage agreements, local marketing agreements, or similar arrangements between full power and low power stations would be prohibited. No individual or entity would be allowed to own more than one low power FM or microradio station in the same community — though the NPRM sought comment on the proper definition of "market" and "community." It also sought comment on whether cross ownership by low power FM licensees of other media outlets, such as television stations, cable television systems, and newspapers, should be allowed.

The Commission then turned to the issue of a national ownership cap. It tentatively decided there was no reason to restrict the number of low power FM stations one person or entity could own nationally. It did seek comment on whether a five- or 10-station limit might be proper. However, it surmised that no limit would be preferable because the efficiencies of owning multiple facilities might spur the growth of this service.

A residency requirement for low power FM owners was also tentatively rejected. Such a requirement has never been found to be an essential component of addressing local needs and interests in full service broadcasting. However, the restriction against alien ownership of full power stations found in 47 U.S.C. Sec. 310 will apply to low power FM as well.

Character qualification rules and restrictions against unauthorized broadcasters were tentatively favored by the Commission. There is a special wrinkle with regard to unauthorized broadcasters. The Commission must decide whether current and/or previously unlicensed broadcasters should be allowed to apply for a new low power FM frequency. It sought comment on whether those who have persistently engaged in unlawful operation should be declared *per se* unqualified to operate a low power FM facility and, if so, whether they should be allowed to rehabilitate themselves so they may apply in the future.

Other Issues

Service characteristics were the next issue addressed by the NPRM. Some commenters had sought a minimum local programming origination requirement, arguing that listeners benefit from local programming since it often reflects their needs, interests, circumstances, or perspectives that may be unique to that community. The Commission declined to impose such a requirement. However, it emphasized that low power FM stations will not be permitted to act as translators for full power stations.

The NPRM also sought comment on whether low power FM stations should be restricted to noncommercial operation, tentatively deciding against this result. It noted that LP1000 stations might need to generate revenue to sustain operations, but LP100 stations might sell some form of advertising to subsidize their operation while also providing an advertising alternative for neighborhood businesses that could not afford to advertise on full power stations.

The Commission did state it expects low power FM stations to adhere to the same public interest programming requirements imposed upon full power stations. LP1000 stations would have to air programming responsive to the community and would have to comply with rules regulating lotteries and sponsorship announcements, the personal attack rules, and rules requiring periodic call sign announcements. These rules are not proposed for LP100 and microradio stations.

Other rules applying to full service broadcasters would also apply to LP1000 stations, including main studio, public file, and ownership reporting requirements. The Commission did not propose to apply these rules to microradio stations. It sought comment on whether these rules should apply to LP100 stations.

The Commission tentatively concluded in the NPRM that its minimum operating hours requirement for full power stations should be imposed on LP1000 stations as well, proposing that LP1000 stations operate for at least two-thirds of their authorized hours between 6 a.m. and midnight. No minimum operating requirement was proposed for LP100 and microradio stations.

The Commission also struggled with the amount of time allowed for stations to construct their facilities. It eventually proposed construction periods that would vary with the class of the service and the complexity of the facilities. LP100 stations would have an 18-month period in which to construct facilities or lose the construction permit. The construction period would be 12 months for microradio stations. LP1000 stations would have the same construction period as full power stations — three years.

Online Application Process

The final issue discussed in the NPRM was the application process. The Commission tentatively concluded all applications should be filed electronically for fear that paper applications would overwhelm Commission staff. It sought to avoid the problem that arose when the low power television service was created. A partial freeze was imposed after more than 37,000 applications became backlogged; the majority of authorized stations still have not been constructed. The Commission did not believe electronic filing would impose a substantial burden on applicants, as interested parties would have access to the Internet through a variety of sources.

The proposed system would entail applicants filing applications via electronic mail. These applications would be analyzed against existing facilities and previously filed applications; the applicant would then be told whether the frequency is available and the application acceptable for filing. The NPRM tentatively concluded that filing windows of a few days each would be more efficient than a first-come, first-served process. This would create situations in which mutually exclusive applications would exist for given frequencies. Though auctions are not required to resolve these mutual exclusivity problems, the Commission sought comment on whether auctions would be a proper method for resolving these conflicts.

Comments in this proceeding were originally due April 12, 1999, with reply comments due on May 12, 1999. These deadlines were extended on numerous occasions. The final comment deadline was Aug. 2, 1999. The reply comment deadline was extended several more times before reply comments were finally due on Nov. 5, 1999. Because of this delay, a Report and Order adopting final rules was not released until Jan. 27, 2000. An article describing the final rules for low power FM radio will appear in the next edition of this publication.

— **Richard M. Schmidt, Jr. and Kevin M. Goldberg**

F. FCC Proposes Mandates for 'Video Descriptions' for Broadcast and Cable Programming

In November 1999 the Federal Communications Commission proposed new rules to require commercial television broadcasters in the top 25 television markets, and the largest national video programming distributors, to include "video descriptions" in their programs to assist persons with visual disabilities. *In the Matter of Implementation of Video Description of Video Programming, Notice of Proposed Rulemaking, MM Docket No. 99-339,* FCC 99-353 (released Nov. 18, 1999) ("NPRM" or "Notice"). The descriptions insert narrations of settings and actions not otherwise reflected in dialogue into TV programs, such as the movement of persons in the scene. They are typically transmitted through the secondary audio programming (SAP) channel and are audible only when that channel is activated using a television or VCR with SAP capability.

FCC Proposal

The FCC Notice asked for comment on a proposal that the initial video description rules require broadcast network affiliates in the top 25 television markets to provide a minimum of 50 hours per calendar quarter (roughly four hours per week) of described prime time and/or children's programming no later than 18 months from the effective date of its video description rules. The NPRM also sought comment on requiring larger video programming distributors to carry the described programming of the broadcasters affiliated with the top four networks, as well as that of non-broadcast networks that reach 50 percent or more of multichannel video programming distributor (MVPD) households.

The FCC also proposed applying the rules eventually to all video programming distributors, including TV broadcast stations, cable operators, direct broadcast satellite (DBS) operators, home satellite dish providers, open video system (OVS) operators, satellite master antenna television (SMATV) operators, and wireless cable operators using multichannel multipoint distribution service (MMDS) channels. Although the FCC is proposing to initially limit the video description rules to analog broadcasters, it noted that it intends to apply the requirements to digital broadcasters in the future.

This latest Notice follows two earlier FCC studies of video description — a July 1996 report following a Notice of Inquiry on closed captioning and video description, and a January 1998 report included in the FCC's annual report to Congress on competition in the market for video programming. The proposed video description rules are generally modeled after the existing closed captioning rules. But because video description technology is not as developed as closed captioning technology, the FCC stated that it would proceed incrementally to implement video description requirements. Incremental or not, the Commission made clear its intention "to increase the amount of required described programming over time ... in order to ensure the accessibility of video programming to persons with visual impairments," as envisioned by Congress in Section 713(f) of the Act. Notice, at ¶ 21.

Statutory Background

The statutory authority upon which the FCC proposes to rely for its video description proposal is somewhat mysterious. Section 713 of the Telecommunications Act of 1996 required the FCC to establish a schedule of deadlines for the provision of closed captioning of video programming. 47 U.S.C.A. Sec. 713(c) (West Supp. 1997). Pursuant to this mandate, the FCC adopted rules for the implementation of closed captioning in 1997. (See *The First Amendment and the Media - 1998,* at pp. 53-56.)

The Telecommunication Act's approach to video description requirements was markedly different. Rather than authorizing or requiring rules to implement video descriptions, the 1996 Act required the FCC only to conduct an inquiry into the use of video descriptions on video programming and to report its findings to Congress. The House version of the bill had provided that, following the inquiry into video descriptions, the FCC could adopt regulations it deemed necessary to promote the accessibility of video programming to persons with visual impairments. But this authorization for FCC action ultimately was not adopted, and the conference report noted that the final legislation deleted the House provision referencing Commission rulemaking authority with respect to video description.

Recognizing that the 1996 Act contains no mandate for video description rules, the Commission's Notice points to a "general legislative preference for the increased accessibility of certain communications services for persons with disabilities" and describes as "potentially relevant" the video description inquiry required by Section 713 of the Telecommunications Act. Otherwise, the Notice appears to find authority to adopt video description rules in the Communications Act's general public interest mandate, the FCC's general authority to make rules, its jurisdiction over "all interstate and foreign communication by wire or radio," and its mandate "to make available, so far as possible, to all the people of the United States ... a rapid, efficient, Nation-wide, and world-wide wire and radio communication service."

In short, the FCC's position appears to be that the agency is empowered to adopt any regulation of content for the media under its jurisdiction that it believes would serve the public interest.

Under this approach, the Commission would have such authority even for rules that were considered, but rejected, by Congress. And its suggestion that the general statutory mandate to serve all the people of the United States creates authority for video description rules would similarly justify FCC rules requiring bilingual broadcasting, among a host of other possible policies. Such a statutory interpretation gives the FCC almost limitless authority to regulate content in the electronic media.

Constitutional Considerations

Whether or not the FCC's statutory analysis is valid, any rule that requires video descriptions by broadcasters and other programming providers would be subject to First Amendment scrutiny. Just as the First Amendment limits the government's ability to restrict what a person can say, it also prevents the government from forcing an unwilling speaker to communicate. As the Supreme Court has emphasized, "'[s]ince *all* speech inherently involves choices of what to say and what to leave unsaid,' one important manifestation of the principle of free speech is that one who chooses to speak may also decide 'what not to say.'" *Hurley v. Irish-American Gay, Lesbian, and Bisexual Group of Boston*, 515 U.S. 557, 573 (1995) (emphasis in original) (quotation omitted).

The Court has made clear that "the First Amendment guarantees 'freedom of speech,' a term necessarily comprising the decision of both what to say and what not to say." *Riley v. National Federation of the Blind of N.C., Inc.*, 487 U.S. 781, 796-97 (1988). See also *Wooley v. Maynard*, 430 U.S. 705, 714 (1977) ("the right of freedom of thought protected by the First Amendment against state action includes both the right to speak freely and the right to refrain from speaking at all"). The Court has rejected the argument that the government may compel statements of fact rather than opinion, noting that "either form of compulsion burdens protected speech." *Riley*, 487 U.S. at 797-98.

The compelled speech question presented by video description rules is even more significant than the one posed by closed captioning rules. With closed captions, the producer or distributor of a program is required to provide existing dialogue in visual form. But with video description, the producer would be required to create material that was never before part of the prior work and to alter the program to conform with federal regulations. Such a legal requirement to write new material and to modify creative works is without precedent in American law.

The constitutional issues seem evident when considering the application of such rules to the print medium. Few would suggest, for example, that the federal government constitutionally could order the *New York Times* to produce a Braille edition, however meritorious that might be. Yet such obvious First Amendment problems often are overlooked when the proposed regulation involves regulated electronic media.

Broadcasters, who would be the initial targets of video description rules, historically have been accorded less First Amendment protection under *Red Lion Broadcasting Co. v. FCC*, 395 U.S. 367 (1969), and other cases. Nevertheless, there are no judicial precedents that address directly whether the FCC constitutionally could require the creation of new programming material, as would be required with video description. Moreover, even under *Red Lion*, the FCC's ability to impose programming mandates is not unlimited. Courts repeatedly have noted that the Commission must "walk a 'tightrope' to preserve the First Amendment values written into the Radio Act and its successor, the Communications Act." *CBS, Inc. v. Democratic National Committee*, 412 U.S. 94, 117 (1973); *Banzhaf v. FCC*, 405 F.2d 1082, 1095 (D.C. Cir. 1968), *cert. denied sub nom. Tobacco Institute, Inc. v. FCC*, 396 U.S. 842 (1969).

The Supreme Court described this balancing act as "a task of great delicacy and difficulty." *CBS, Inc.*, 412 U.S. at 102, and stressed that "we would [not] hesitate to invoke the Constitution should we determine that the [FCC] has not fulfilled with appropriate sensitivity to the interest of free expression." In this context, specific program requirements have always been considered the most constitutionally suspect. The D.C. Circuit has emphasized that the "power to specify material which the public interest requires or forbids to be broadcast ... carries the seeds of the general authority to censor denied by the Communications Act and the First Amendment alike." *Banzhaf*, 405 F.2d at 1095. Public interest requirements relating to specific program content "must be closely scrutinized lest they carry the Commission too far in the direction of the forbidden censorship." *Id.* at 1096.

In *Turner Broadcasting System, Inc. v. FCC*, 515 U.S. 622 (1994), the Supreme Court emphasized "the minimal extent" that the government may influence the programming provided by broadcast stations, and the Court made clear that "the FCC's oversight responsibilities do not grant it the power to ordain any particular type of programming that must be offered by broadcast stations." *Id.* at 650. And to whatever extent such authority existed in the past, it is uncertain that the same power will continue in perpetuity. The Supreme Court has noted that "because the broadcast industry is dynamic in terms of technological change[,] solutions adequate a decade ago are not necessarily so now, and those acceptable today may well be outmoded ten years hence." *CBS, Inc.*, 412 U.S. at 102. And, as Chief Judge Richard S. Arnold of the U.S. Court of Appeals for the Eighth Circuit has noted:

> There is something about a government order compelling someone to utter or repeat speech that rings legal alarm bells. The Supreme Court believed, almost twenty-five years ago, that broadcasting was sufficiently special to overcome this instinctive feeling of alarm. There is a good chance that the legal landscape has changed enough since that time to produce a different result. *Arkansas AFL-CIO v. FCC*, 11 F.3d 1430, 1443 (8th Cir. 1993) (en banc) (Arnold, C.J., concurring).

See also *Syracuse Peace Council v. FCC*, 867 F.2d 654, 684-85 (D.C. Cir. 1989), *cert. denied*, 493 U.S. 1019 (1990) (Starr, J., concurring) (*Red Lion* has been undermined by technological and market developments).

Even if video description rules could be supported as applied to traditional broadcast stations, the FCC has indicated its intention to impose the requirements eventually on "all distributors of video programming over which we have jurisdiction." Notice, at ¶ 24. In this regard, the Supreme Court has stated categorically that "the rationale for applying a less rigorous standard of First Amendment scrutiny to broadcast regulation, whatever its validity in the cases elaborating it, does not apply in the context of cable regulation." Noting the "fundamental technological differences between broadcast and cable transmission," the Court found that application of "the more relaxed standard of scrutiny adopted in *Red Lion* and the other broadcast cases is inapt when determining the First Amendment validity of cable regulation." *Turner*, 512 U.S. at 639. The Court in *Turner* stressed that "[a]t the heart of the First Amendment lies the principle that each person should decide for him- or herself the ideas and beliefs deserving of expression" and that regulation that "requires the utterance of a particular message favored by the Government, contravenes this essential right." *Id.* at 641. The same constitutional considerations apply equally to other non-broadcast media.

The constitutional issues raised by the proposed video description rules are significant, and perhaps all the more so in that the First Amendment issues were not mentioned at all in the FCC's Notice of Proposed Rulemaking.

—Robert Corn-Revere

G. FCC Opens Inquiry on Public Interest Obligations of Digital TV Broadcasters in Wake of Gore Commission

On Dec. 18, 1998, the president's Advisory Committee on Public Interest Obligations of Digital Television Broadcasters (popularly known as the Gore Commission) issued its final report. See *Charting the Digital Broadcasting Future: Final Report of the Advisory Committee on Public Interest Obligations of Digital Television Broadcasters*, available at <www.ntia.doc.gov/pubintadvcom/pubint.htm>. The report's recommendations for 10 additional public interest obligations for digital television (DTV) broadcasters were described last year in *The First Amendment and the Media - 1999.*

At the time of the report's release it received little attention, though a few members of Congress expressed some interest in introducing legislation based on Gore Commission recommendations. See "Lieberman ponders digital TV public interest bill," *Broadcasting & Cable*, April 12, 1999, at 22. Then in June 1999, People for Better TV, describing itself as a "broad coalition of concerned citizens and organizations," filed with the Federal Communications Commission a Petition for Rule Making and a Petition for Notice of Inquiry seeking "an inquiry into, and the establishment of clear guidelines regarding, the public interest responsibilities of digital television broadcasters."

On Oct. 20, Vice President Gore submitted a letter to the chairman of the FCC asking the Commission to initiate a public proceeding regarding digital television broadcasters to address four issues: the need for higher quality political discourse; disaster warnings in the digital age; disability access to digital programming; and diversity in broadcasting (programming, employment, and ownership diversity). Letter from Vice President Al Gore to William E. Kennard, chairman, FCC, Oct. 20, 1999.

The FCC Reacts

The FCC undertook such a proceeding in December 1999. *In the Matter of Public Interest Obligations of TV Broadcast Licensees, Notice of Inquiry, MM Docket No. 99-360*, FCC 99-390 (adopted Dec. 15, 1999) ("NOI" or "Notice"). The premise of the Notice is that "[t]elevision is the primary source of news and information to Americans, and provides hours of entertainment every week." Therefore, "[g]iven the impact of their programming and their use of the public airwaves, broadcasters have a special role in serving the public." Notice, at ¶ 1.

Moreover, digital television technology provides new opportunities for "reinventing free, over-the-air television" through high definition programming, the ability to "multicast," and the ability to "datacast." *Id.* at ¶ 3. In seeking comments on "how broadcasters can best serve the public interest during and after the transition to digital technology," *id.* at ¶ 9, the Notice relies extensively on both the Gore Commission final report and the petition of People for Better TV.

First the FCC seeks comment on how, generally, public interest obligations should apply to broadcasters that multicast or provide ancillary and supplementary services. *Id.* at ¶¶ 10-13. Then, the first group of issues — "Responding to the Community" — cites as one fundamental public interest obligation a broadcaster's need to air programming responsive to the needs and interests of its local community. *Id.* at ¶ 14. Thus the Notice seeks comment on ascertainment requirements and requirements that broadcasters make enhanced disclosures of their public interest programming and activities. Another such obligation on which comment is sought is how broadcasters can warn viewers about impending disasters and keep them informed about related events. *Id.* at ¶ 19. And the FCC seeks comment on the debate fostered by the Gore Commission final report as to whether the agency should adopt mandatory minimum public interest requirements or rely on marketplace incentives to produce adequate local programming and meet community needs. *Id.* at ¶ 22.

Under the heading "Enhancing Access to the Media," the FCC quotes the final report in asking for comment on how the new digital technologies can provide "maximum choice and quality for Americans with disabilities" — for example, through enhanced closed captioning and more widely available video description. *Id.* at ¶ 25. Although acknowledging a number of initiatives that broadcasters already are pursuing voluntarily to foster diversity, the NOI stresses a fundamental public policy goal of increasing "[d]iversity of viewpoint, ownership, and employment," and inquires about additional measures in this regard. *Id.* at ¶¶ 29, 33.

Finally, the NOI address "Enhancing Political Discourse," the primary, contentious issue that launched the Gore Commission. While proposing no rules or policies in the Notice itself, the FCC's goal is to "initiate a public debate on the question of whether, and how, broadcasters' public interest obligations can be refined to promote democracy and better educate the voting public." *Id.* at ¶ 34. Here the Notice both mentions the increased voluntary efforts by some broadcasters and the scant and shrinking coverage of local public affairs by others.

The Notice refers to the Gore Commission's consensus recommendation for broadcasters to voluntarily provide five minutes each night at election time for "candidate-centered discourse," and the proposals of a majority of that Commission, and others, that go well beyond this to specific requirements that television broadcasters provide airtime for national and local candidates. *Id.* at ¶¶ 37-38. The FCC seeks comment on its authority to impose such mandates and to prohibit broadcasters from adopting blanket bans on the sale of airtime to state and local candidates.

Notably, the Notice says nothing about the justifications or rationales for any of the proposals on which it seeks comment. There is no mention of the First Amendment or suggestion that there are any constitutional issues for commenters to address.

Commissioner Furchtgott-Roth's Dissent

Com. Harold Furchtgott-Roth, however, noted that he thought most of the NOI's proposals lacked merit. He concurred in the NOI only in part and dissented in part. In his Separate Statement he first was disturbed by the NOI's "vast breadth, often musing about public interest mandates that have no discernible nexus to the transition to digital technology" but seem to be just the product of "special interests" seeking to "wring as many concessions as possible out of broadcasters." The "Notice dreams of creating a new Great DTV Society," and it seeks to "cure virtually every social ill through the mandated largesse of broadcasters," but with "little regard for the nature of our statutory authority ... or the limits imposed by the Constitution."

Second, the NOI is "remarkably out-of-step with today's communications marketplace.... The Commission's rules should be moving toward deregulation, not further burdening the emergence" of digital television. If the spectrum scarcity rationale for regulation is no longer viable as a factual matter, then any additional regulation of broadcasting will be "highly problematic in constitutional terms."

Third, Com. Furchtgott-Roth expressed his discomfort with "this *independent* agency taking its 'guidance' and 'focus' from an executive branch Committee and the Vice President on issues that are exclusively within our jurisdiction." He objects to the FCC's ceding guidance of the NOI to the "Administration's policy wish list" reflected in the Gore Commission's final report because doing so "undermine[s] the very core of our mission as an agency."

Public comments on the NOI are due March 27, 2000, and reply comments April 25. These comments are sure to be highly contentious.

— **Laurence H. Winer**

COMMERCIAL SPEECH

COMMERCIAL SPEECH

The Media Institute and its First Amendment Advisory Council graded the three branches of the federal government and state and local government for their support of the First Amendment regarding the above commercial speech issues as follows:

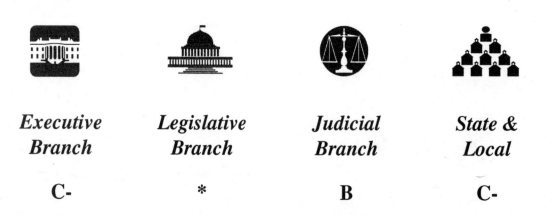

Executive Branch	*Legislative Branch*	*Judicial Branch*	*State & Local*
C-	*	B	C-

*No Legislative Branch developments in commercial speech.

A. Commercial Speech Fares Well in Federal Courts but Protection Lags at State Level

This year saw increased protection for commercial speech, particularly in the federal courts. However, state courts did not follow the federal trend in 1999 and continued to be significantly less protective of commercial speech.

Tenth Circuit Strikes FCC Privacy Regulations

A recent federal court decision illustrates the generally protective approach of the federal courts to commercial speech. The U.S. Court of Appeals for the Tenth Circuit invalidated, on First Amendment grounds, Federal Communications Commission regulations restricting use, disclosure, and access regarding customer proprietary network information (CPNI). *U.S. West, Inc. v. FCC*, 182 F.3d 1224 (10th Cir. 1999).

The FCC promulgated these regulations to implement a section of the Telecommunications Act of 1996 requiring telecommunications carriers to protect the confidentiality of CPNI. In essence, the regulations permitted telecommunications carriers to use, disclose, or share CPNI "for the purpose of marketing products within a category of service" that the customer already subscribed to. *Id*. at 1230. However, the regulations prohibited carriers from disclosing or permitting access to CPNI for the purpose of marketing to the customer categories of service to which the customer did not already subscribe, unless the customer had approved of such disclosure.

The government argued that these regulations did not restrict speech because they allowed carriers to communicate with their customers, even though they prohibited carriers from using CPNI to "target" customers. The court rejected this argument, stating that "[e]ffective speech has two components: a speaker and an audience. A restriction on either of these components is a restriction on speech." *Id*. at 1232. The court next determined that the regulations restricted truthful, nonmisleading commercial speech.

In determining whether the restriction violated the First Amendment, the court applied the test established by the Supreme Court in *Central Hudson Gas & Electric Corp. v. Public Service*

Commission, 447 U.S. 557 (1980). The court assumed — with some reservations — that the government's interest in protecting consumer privacy was substantial. It declined, however, to find the government's interest — standing alone — in promoting competition substantial because the specific statutory section at issue was not a competition section, but rather a privacy section.

The court then found that the regulation did not materially and directly advance the government's interests because the government had failed to present any evidence that the asserted harms of disclosure were real. The court did consider whether the regulations were narrowly tailored, assuming, *arguendo*, that the regulations directly advanced the government's substantial interests. It determined that they were not because the government had failed to demonstrate that a less restrictive method of protecting privacy would have been ineffective.

Hostile Rulings by California, Pennsylvania Courts

By contrast, state courts have been significantly more hostile toward commercial speech, as two recent opinions illustrate. In *Keimer v. Buena Vista Books, Inc.*, 89 Cal. Rptr. 2d 781 (1999), a California state appellate court determined that advertising statements made on book and videotape covers (*i.e.*, jackets) were commercial speech rather than noncommercial speech entitled to full free speech protection. The court held that the book covers were advertisements, that they referred to a specific product, and that the drafter had an economic motivation in making the statements. Based on this analysis, the court concluded that the speech was commercial. Next, the court determined that the speech did not merit protection under *Central Hudson* because it was false and misleading. With that, the court ended its cursory inquiry.

Similarly, the Pennsylvania Supreme Court declined to protect speech in *Commonwealth v. State Board of Physical Therapy*, 728 A.2d 340 (Pa. 1999), when it ruled that a law prohibiting chiropractors from advertising physical therapy services does not violate the First Amendment. The court focused on the fact that the chiropractors to whom the law applies are not licensed physical therapists, nor do they employ licensed physical therapists. The court stated that "commercial speech such as advertising enjoys limited constitutional protection and can be regulated in a more stringent manner than non-commercial speech." *Id*. at 343. It then ruled that "[t]he principle that misleading or deceptive advertising may be prohibited is ... dispositive of this case" because "[a]llowing chiropractors to advertise that they perform 'physical therapy' would mislead the public into believing that chiropractors are actually licensed and able to perform the full range of such therapy." *Id*. at 344.

Massachusetts Cigar Regulations Challenged

A pending federal case worthy of monitoring by First Amendment advocates is *Lorillard Tobacco Co. v. Reilly*.[1] In that case, cigar and tobacco manufacturers and retailers have challenged Massachusetts regulations that seek to impose numerous restrictions on the sale of cigars, including product placement and labeling requirements. The labeling requirements direct each manufacturer, packager, importer for sale, or distributor of cigars to label its cigars and cigar advertisements in a prescribed manner. In November 1999, certain plaintiffs moved for partial summary judgment on First Amendment grounds.

On Jan. 24, 2000, the court rejected all but one of the tobacco companies' First Amendment arguments and ruled that the tobacco and cigar regulations are valid exercises of the attorney general's authority. Although the court agreed with the tobacco companies that the speech at issue is commercial speech, it rejected the argument that a standard more protective of speech than *Central Hudson* should apply. The court distinguished *Carey v. Population Services International*, 431 U.S. 678 (1977), and reasoned that the negative social effects of tobacco products prevent greater protection from applying. Additionally, the court ruled that, unlike *Carey*, the Massachusetts regulations do not totally suppress all advertising.

Applying the *Central Hudson* test, the court assumed, without deciding, that the targeted speech would qualify for constitutional protection. Next, the court found that Massachusetts has a substantial government interest in preventing underage smoking, and that the regulations directly advance the government's interest — based upon the mere "common-sense connection between promotional advertising and consumption." Opinion, at 14. Finally, the court ruled that the outdoor advertising restrictions are not more extensive than necessary to serve the government interest, but that the point-of-sale advertising provisions are more extensive than necessary because the government "never delineated what the proper zone would be, if any, for regulation of *indoor* advertisements." *Id.* at 31 (emphasis in original). The court severed the point-of-sale restriction and allowed the outdoor advertising restrictions to stand. The court did rule, however, that cigar advertisements in national magazines and in other national media are exempt from the regulations' warning requirements.

— **Daniel E. Troy**

---

[1] The author of this section, Daniel E. Troy, is a partner at the law firm of Wiley, Rein & Fielding, which represents Brown & Williamson Tobacco Corp. in this action.

B. Supreme Court Upholds First Amendment Protection for Casino Gambling Commercials

Free speech advocates won a significant victory on June 14, 1999 when a unanimous U.S. Supreme Court decided *Greater New Orleans Broadcasting Association v. United States*, 119 S. Ct. 1923 (1999). *Greater New Orleans* held that the First Amendment protects broadcast advertisements for casino gambling and gambling-related activities when those advertisements are broadcast from states that permit such gaming activities. Writing for the Court, Justice John Paul Stevens ruled that 18 U.S.C. Sec. 1304 and its implementing regulations violate the First Amendment because they improperly restrict commercial speech.[1]

Although the case was decided on narrow grounds, the decision heightens the protection afforded commercial speech under the Court's *Central Hudson* analysis. *Central Hudson Gas & Electric Corp. v. Public Service Commission*, 447 U.S. 557 (1980). The Court acknowledged that *Central Hudson* has been sharply criticized by those who argue that the Court should implement "a more straightforward and stringent test for assessing the validity of governmental restrictions on commercial speech." *Greater New Orleans*, 119 S. Ct. at 1930. Stopping short of endorsing or repudiating *Central Hudson*, the Court observed that "there is no need to break new ground" where, as here, "*Central Hudson* ... provides an adequate basis for decision." *Id.*

The case arose when a broadcasters association and others challenged the government's enforcement of a statute that prohibited the broadcast of advertisements for casino gambling. The broadcasters operate in a state where gambling is legal, but their broadcast signals reach into a neighboring state where gambling is illegal. The government claimed that, because the signals reached into a state where gambling is illegal, the advertising was forbidden by 18 U.S.C. Sec. 1304 which prohibits — subject to a number of exceptions — certain radio and television stations from broadcasting "any advertisement of or information concerning any lottery, gift, or similar scheme, offering prizes dependent in whole or in part upon lot or chance...."

Central Hudson Test Applied

The Court found that the content of the broadcast was not misleading and concerned lawful activities. It further held that the government demonstrated substantial interests served by the speech restrictions, namely, reducing the social costs associated with gambling and assisting states that prohibit gambling. However, the Court observed that the government's interest "is by no means self-evident" in light of the fact that "the federal policy of discouraging gambling ... is now decidedly equivocal." *Greater New Orleans*, 119 S. Ct. at 1931-32.

The Court then found that the restriction did not satisfy Parts 3 and 4 of *Central Hudson*. It assumed the validity of the government's "first asserted interest — alleviating the social costs of casino gambling by limiting demand." *Id*. at 1932. However, it ruled that the ban did not directly or materially further the asserted interests because: (1) much of the advertising could "merely channel gamblers to one casino rather than another," *id*. at 1932-33; (2) the government's attempt to minimize the social costs of gambling was not effective in light of Congress's other policies on gambling, *id*. at 1933; and (3) the government failed to "connect casino gambling and compulsive gambling with broadcast advertising for casinos," *id*. The Court dismissed the government's second asserted interest of "'assisting' States with policies that disfavor private casinos." *Id*. at 1935. The Court found that "[Section] 1304 sacrifices an intolerable amount of truthful speech about lawful conduct when compared to all of the policies at stake...." *Id*.

Central to the Court's decision was the fact that Section 1304's policy against gambling is riddled with exceptions that permit gambling and advertising about gambling. For instance, Section 1304 allows advertisements of state-conducted lotteries where the radio or television station is licensed in a state that conducts a lottery. Congress also passed additional statutes that curtail Section 1304. For example, the Indian Gaming Regulatory Act of 1988 authorizes certain Native American tribes to conduct casino gambling and it permits radio and television stations to broadcast advertisements of that gambling. Also, the 1992 Professional and Amateur Sports Protection Act permits many forms of sports betting and advertising of that betting. These exceptions, the Court said, undermine the government's claim that the regulation directly advances the government's interests and is not more extensive than necessary to serve those interests.

Justice Thomas concurred in the judgment. In doing so he reaffirmed his belief, first announced in *44 Liquormart, Inc. v. Rhode Island*, 517 U.S. 484, 518 (1996) (concurring in part and concurring in the judgment), that commercial speech should be granted the same protection as noncommercial speech. Thus, to Justice Thomas, the *Central Hudson* test should not be applied in cases such as this where "the government's asserted interest is to keep legal users of a product or service ignorant in order to manipulate their choices in the marketplace." *Greater New Orleans*, 119 S. Ct. at 1936.

— **Daniel E. Troy**

---

[1] This decision does not affect the Supreme Court's earlier decision in *United States v. Edge Broadcasting Co.*, 509 U.S. 418 (1993), which held that 18 U.S.C. Sec. 1304's restriction on broadcasts from non-lottery states does not violate the First Amendment.

C. Federal Trade Commission Steps Up Internet Oversight, Adopts Rules To Protect Kids' Online Privacy

Few recent issues have caught the attention of the American people — and of Congress — as comprehensively as privacy. As digital media gain ever more advanced capabilities to collect and store information, concerns about the average person's ability to maintain her personal privacy have increased. A new vocabulary for the collection of personal information has been created, with terms such as "data mining" and "online profiling." And few Americans have been seen as vulnerable as children.

In 1998, Congress passed the Children's Online Privacy Protection Act, or COPPA, which was meant to require parental consent to the collection of personally identifiable information about children online (over the Internet or via proprietary online services such as America Online). In 1999, the Federal Trade Commission adopted rules to implement COPPA. It also took actions to hold Web site operators to their posted privacy policies, finding it a deceptive trade practice to vary from those policies. Private litigation, too, began to spring up over more sophisticated practices for the collection of data from Internet users.

FTC Implementation of COPPA

The rules adopted by the FTC in October 1999 require any operator of a Web site or online service directed to children, or any operator that has actual knowledge that it is collecting or maintaining personal information obtained from a child, to comply with certain notice and consent requirements. The FTC's rules provide that COPPA will apply not only to "children's" Web sites such as Nickelodeon (www.nick.com) or Disney (www.disney.com). COPPA will, under the FTC's rules, apply even to general purpose Web sites if the FTC finds — based on a subjective interpretation of the "overall character" of the Web site, including the site's visual or audio content, whether it uses animated characters, or contains child-oriented activities — that any portion of the Web site has been directed at children.

Moreover, any non-child-directed site that has gained actual knowledge that a child has used its site will be deemed to be on notice that it may have collected a child's personal information. The FTC noted that it would examine closely those Web sites that do not ask users to reveal age information at all but do ask for related information that could tell operators they are dealing with a child. If a general purpose Web site gains actual knowledge that it has collected personal information from even one child, it will be required to design its entire information gathering procedures to comply with COPPA.

The FTC's rules also make it clear that COPPA will apply not only to Web sites that actually seek information from children but also to sites where the child himself can supply personally identifiable information. For example, if a child in a child-oriented chat room posts identifying information in a real-time chat, the operator of that Web site will be deemed to have "collected" that personal information from the child.

The net effect of such a ruling, many groups believe, is to require any child-oriented chat rooms and bulletin boards to either close down or adopt 24-hour monitoring to immediately remove any personal information posted by children. The American Library Association, the ACLU, and the Center for Democracy and Technology have urged a more workable reading of this rule. Under this interpretation, an operator of a Web site that does not seek to collect personal information but merely provides a bulletin board, personal home page, or other communications services available to children would not be deemed to be "collecting" information within the meaning of COPPA. Industry groups were discussing these issues with FTC staff at the close of 1999.

If COPPA is found to apply to a Web site or online service, that service is required to take several steps. First, it must post a "clear, prominent, and understandable" privacy notice. The FTC detailed in its rules the information that must be included in such a notice, including what information is collected, how it will be used, and to whom it may be disclosed. Second, it must obtain "verifiable parental consent" for the collection, use, or disclosure of personal information from children. COPPA defines "verifiable parental consent" as "any reasonable effort (taking into consideration available technology)" to ensure parental authorization.

The FTC listed several possible ways operators could obtain this consent, including requiring a parent to mail the operator a consent form or to call a toll-free telephone number. Until April 2002, the FTC will permit consent by e-mail, provided that this method is accompanied by "additional steps ... to provide assurances that the parent is providing the consent." Third, it must provide opportunities for parents to review and delete their child's personal information, must limit collection of personal information to that necessary for the activity, and must protect the integrity of the personal information collected.

FTC Enforcement of Privacy Policies

There currently is no federal or state law that requires Web site operators to post "privacy policies" — statements that provide Web site users with notice of the type of information collected by the site, who will have access to that information, how information will be used and can be corrected, and whether third parties unrelated to the Web site operator will be given access to that information. But consumer concern for privacy, and congressional promises to regulate privacy if the Internet industry does not adopt sufficient self-regulatory measures, has led to an industry practice of posting privacy policies on the majority of popular Web sites.

But posting a voluntary privacy policy is not entirely an unregulated activity. In the GeoCities case in 1998, the FTC found that a Web site operator's failure to comply with the terms of its voluntarily posted privacy policy was a deceptive trade practice. The FTC continued to apply that principle in 1999, finding that the "Young Investors" Web site maintained by Liberty Financial of Boston falsely promised Internet users that information collected from them would be held anonymously. In fact, the site asked children to answer survey questions about allowance amounts, gifts of stocks and bonds, and other financial matters "anonymously" but maintained the information in a way that identified it with each child who responded. The FTC and Liberty Financial entered into a consent decree based on the terms of COPPA. Robert Pitofsky, FTC chairman, cited the decree as another example of the FTC's efforts to protect online privacy and said the FTC is "committed to pursuing law enforcement actions in appropriate cases."

"Online Profiling" Leads to FTC Inquiries

The new practice of "online profiling" involves the recording of online behavior for the production of tailored advertisements or other content. For example, many (if not most) Web sites leave "cookies" on users' computers. These cookies are small text files from which a site can garner innocuous information — for instance, the next time a visitor arrives at a site that previously left a cookie on her computer, the site will know that she is a repeat visitor and may know some information about how she used the site on previous visits. New technology, however, has permitted sites to form ad hoc memberships so that they can read one anothers' cookies. Using these new technologies, for example, a Web site that sells music would be able to tell from a first-time visitor's cookies that she has visited other sites dedicated to classical music. Rather than providing this visitor with a screen promoting jazz, it will provide her with a screen dedicated to classical music.

In late 1999, calls for legislation to control online profiling led the FTC and the Department of Commerce to hold a joint workshop on the legal issues raised by the practice. Those advocating legal restrictions on profiling pointed out that Internet users often use the medium for its supposed anonymity, and that online profiling can reveal such personal data as sexual preference, HIV status, and religious affiliation. Public interest groups pointed out that profiling could lead to "electronic redlining" — the reservation of higher quality online assets to those more likely to be high-dollar customers. No legislative proposals had emerged at the close of the year.

Online profiling has, however, led to private litigation. In late 1999, a lawsuit was filed against Real Networks, Inc., a company that markets software for playing digital audio and video files downloaded from the Internet. The suit alleges that Real Networks configured its software to collect information on users' music preferences in a manner that Real Networks could later collect from its software. The case remains pending without resolution as of this writing.

— Kurt Wimmer

D. Rutgers Grads Take Alumni Magazine to Court in Battle Over Public Forum v. Editorial Discretion

The status of Rutgers University's athletic program has long attracted attention — at least back to the turn-of-the-century antics featured in the 1950s Broadway musical "High Button Shoes." In recent years, however, there has been mounting tension among factions both on and off campus over the proper balance of priorities between academic and athletic pursuits.

Especially vocal has been a group known as the Rutgers 1000 Alumni Council, the principal concern of which has been to reduce the emphasis on big-time intercollegiate sports. The group has been particularly critical of Athletic Director Robert Mulcahy, whom a former Rutgers Board of Trustees chairman describes as "hand picked for the job by Governor Christie Whitman."

The Rutgers 1000 Alumni Council specifically asked the alumni magazine to publish an advertisement that would convey its major concerns to fellow graduates and to the larger university community. The ad would include a statement by Nobel Laureate Milton Friedman, a Rutgers graduate, deploring the alleged lessening of academic priorities at his alma mater. The editor of the magazine adamantly refused to run the ad. With the support of the New Jersey chapter of the American Civil Liberties Union, the Rutgers 1000 filed suit in state court in late April 1999. The suit alleged that the magazine's action abridges the First Amendment rights of the splinter alumni group and its members.

The case raises several difficult issues, comparable in part to those before the Supreme Court two years ago in *Arkansas Educational Television Network v. Forbes*, 523 U.S. 666 (1998). There are free expression interests on both sides — those of the alumni seeking a voice through a state-supported official organ for Rutgers graduates on one hand, and those of the editors on the other hand seeking to exercise editorial judgment on a volatile issue.

The nature of the material is superficially different from the views of Arkansas congressional candidates involved in *Forbes*, since the Rutgers 1000's submission was in the form of a paid advertisement. Yet courts today would almost certainly characterize the statement as an "editorial advertisement" of the type the Supreme Court held fully protected in *New York Times Co. v. Sullivan*, 376 U.S. 254 (1964).

Public Forum Issues

Then there will be difficult public forum issues — whether, despite rejection of forum arguments as to the candidate debate in *Forbes*, a court might be more likely to find the Rutgers alumni magazine to be at least a limited public forum to which all alumni groups should have access without viewpoint or message bias exercised by the university administration. There is in fact a quite analogous New Jersey Supreme Court case, holding in the early 1980s that every gubernatorial candidate had a right to appear on a publicly televised debate (though the basis for that judgment was more statutory than constitutional.)

Finally, there is the issue that proved central in *Forbes* — whether such an action falls within an editor's discretion or judgment to accept or reject controversial material, even at a publicly supported medium. By curious irony, the case most closely in point happened to involve the *Rutgers University Law Review*, whose editors many years ago were held by the U.S. Court of Appeals for the Third Circuit to have acted within the zone of editorial discretion when they rejected an article that expressed an unpopular view on highly sensitive racial issues. *Avins v. Rutgers University*, 385 F.2d 151 (3d Cir. 1967), *cert. denied*, 390 U.S. 920 (1968). While there are obvious differences between Rutgers's law review and its alumni magazine, this precedent could hardly be avoided even if it were not quite so close to home.

Given the intensity of feeling on both sides, and the obvious import of the case, settlement seems highly unlikely. It will probably take some time working its way through the New Jersey courts. Many others than Rutgers alumni will await the outcome with keen anticipation.

— **Robert M. O'Neil**

E. FCC Adopts 'Truth-in-Billing' Rules for Phone Service; Commissioner Questions First Amendment Impact

In May 1999, the Federal Communications Commission adopted rules it said were needed to ensure that consumers receive thorough, accurate, and understandable bills from their telecommunications carriers. *In the Matter of Truth-in-Billing and Billing Format, CC Docket No. 98-170, First Report and Order and Further Notice of Proposed Rulemaking,* FCC 99-72 (released May 11, 1999) ("Order"). The rules require all carriers to identify line-item charges associated with federal regulatory action with a standard industry-wide label, and to provide full, clear, and "non-misleading descriptions" of the nature of the charges.

In a dissenting statement, however, Com. Harold Furchtgott-Roth charged that the underlying motive of the rules was to hide the fact that various federal mandates, such as universal service fund contributions and the e-rate program of subsidies to schools and libraries, result in higher telephone bills for consumers. He described the FCC's Order as "misleading" and said that the rule, which requires telecommunications carriers to use "the government's preferred explanation of the charges," raises "grave First Amendment questions."

Uniform Labels Required

Under the truth-in-billing rules, telecommunications carriers are required, among other things, to use a "brief, clear, non-misleading, plain language description of the service or services rendered." 47 C.F.R. Sec. 64.2001(b). The FCC extended the principle of full and non-misleading descriptions "to carrier charges purportedly associated with federal regulatory action." Order, at ¶ 49. It noted that universal service fund contributions required to support "the universal availability of telecommunications services at just, reasonable, and affordable rates" were variously described on long-distance bills as a "universal connectivity charge," a "federal universal service fee," or a "local service subsidy," among other things.

Similarly, descriptions of access-related charges included "carrier line charge," "national access fee," and "presubscribed line charge." Local carriers who assessed a fee to support number portability pursuant to the dictates of the Telecommunications Act of 1996 variously described the charge on their bills as a "number portability surcharge" or as a "federal charge —

service provider number portability." The Commission found that such descriptions led to consumer confusion in that "[t]he names associated with these charges as well as accompanying descriptions (or entire lack thereof) may convince consumers that all of these fees are federally mandated." *Id.* at ¶ 53. This, in turn, makes it difficult for consumers to compare the prices charged by competing service providers, according to the Order.

Therefore, the Commission adopted its proposed guideline that line-item charges associated with federal regulatory action must be identified through standard and uniform labels across the industry. *Id.* at ¶ 54. Noting that "consumer groups are particularly well-suited to assist in the development of the uniform terms," the FCC issued a further notice of proposed rulemaking seeking comment on what specific description (or label) should be used for each of these charges. Despite requiring uniform labeling, the FCC affirmed that carriers have discretion to decide whether and to what extent to recover these costs from consumers. The Commission also decided that carriers may choose to include additional language elsewhere on the bill describing the charges. *Id.* at ¶ 56.

Different Treatment

The "truth-in-billing" rules contrast sharply with the treatment accorded other regulatory fees, such as cable television franchise fees. Under federal law, local franchising authorities are permitted to charge up to 5 percent of a cable operator's gross revenues as a franchise fee. Like the telecommunications carriers that are subject to the "truth-in-billing" rules, cable operators are permitted, but not required, to pass all or part of the franchise fee on to subscribers in the form of higher rates. However, Section 622(f) of the Cable Act provides that "[a] cable operator may designate that portion of a subscriber's bill attributable to the franchise fee as a separate item on the bill," 47 U.S.C. Sec. 542(f), even though subscribers may reasonably conclude that such charges amount to a "tax" that was "mandated" by local government. Indeed, the purpose underlying Section 622(f) is to ensure that franchising authorities will be accountable to the public.

One difference between cable franchise fees and telecommunications charges is that the universal service fund in general, and the e-rate program to fund computer use in schools and libraries in particular, had become highly politicized. Critics of the e-rate program have described the $2.25 billion in subsidies and associated charges as the "Gore tax," and blamed the increased costs on the vice president. See, *e.g.,* Karen Tumulty and John Dickerson, "Gore's costly high wire act," *Time,* May 25, 1998, at 52. In this highly charged context, six bills were introduced in Congress in 1999 to reduce or entirely eliminate the e-rate program. But in answer to such pressures, FCC Chairman William E. Kennard noted recent surveys showing that 87 percent of Americans support the e-rate program. William E. Kennard, "E-rate: A success story" [address to the Council of Chief State School Officers], Jan. 14, 2000.

First Amendment Concerns

Com. Furchtgott-Roth's concern, as expressed in his dissent in the "truth-in-billing" proceeding, is that consumer protection rules are being used pretextually to preserve public support for a politically divisive program. Noting that "[f]ew politicians welcome the opportunity to be associated with a new tax," he pointed out that "[a]ccountability for charges that some consider a tax is not just a business matter, but a highly political one." Speech that is "fraught with political significance" would be subject to strict First Amendment scrutiny, and not the relatively less rigorous review accorded purely commercial speech. Com. Furchtgott-Roth wrote that under strict scrutiny, the regulations "are presumptively violative of the First Amendment." But he also analyzed the rules under the commercial speech doctrine articulated in *Central Hudson Gas & Electric Corp. v. Public Service Commission*, 447 U.S. 557 (1980), and concluded that the Commission majority had failed to demonstrate that the possibility of consumer confusion is real and not conjectural, that the regulations would materially advance the stated goals, or that the rules were sufficiently narrow.

The Commission concluded that the rules are constitutional under *Central Hudson*. It found that the government has a substantial interest in ensuring that consumers are not misled, and that a "lack of standard labelling could make comparison shopping infeasible." Order, at ¶ 61. The majority also found that the rules would materially advance the stated interest, and that they were no more extensive than necessary because carriers would be required only to use standard labelling and would not be precluded from describing the charges more fully elsewhere on the bill. *Id.* at ¶¶ 62-63. With respect to such descriptions, however, the majority cautioned that "we would not consider a description of [the universal service] charge as being 'mandated' by the Commission or the federal government to be accurate." *Id.* at ¶ 56.

— **Robert Corn-Revere**

F. Federal Court Strikes Down CFTC's Regulation of Investment Advice Publishers

Rules of the Commodity Futures Trading Commission (CFTC) requiring online publishers of investment information to register as "commodity trading advisors" under the Commodity Exchange Act were struck down as a violation of the First Amendment. In *Taucher v. Born*, 53 F. Supp. 2d 464 (D.D.C. 1999), the U.S. District Court for the District of Columbia held that the registration requirement was a direct regulation of speech, that investment advice was entitled to full First Amendment protection, and that the registration requirement, as applied to publishers, imposed a prior restraint on protected speech.

The case involved four publishers whose publications include books, newsletters, Internet Web sites, trading systems, and computer software that provide information, analysis, and advice on commodity futures trading. Several members of the public who read and use the publications also joined in the suit. The plaintiffs filed a constitutional challenge to the CFTC's application of portions of the Commodity Exchange Act, 7 U.S.C. Sec. 1 *et seq.* ("CEA"), which require "investment advisors" who "make use of the mails or any means or instrumentality of interstate commerce" to register with the CFTC.

The law defines a commodity trading advisor as any person who engages in the business of advising others on trading in commodities, either directly or through publications, writings, or electronic media, or who issues analyses or reports on commodities trading. 7 U.S.C. Sec. 1a(5)(A). The definition excludes "the publisher or producer of any print or electronic data of general and regular dissemination" provided that the furnishing of such services "is solely incidental to the conduct of their business or profession," 7 U.S.C. Secs. 1a(5)(B)(iv), 1a(5)(C).

The court noted that "each of the plaintiffs in this case falls squarely within the definition of the CEA," and that the publication exemption did not apply because "the furnishing of such services is the plaintiffs' primary business or profession." *Taucher*, 53 F. Supp. 2d at 475. Accordingly, it found that they were required to register with the CFTC and to satisfy other conditions such as paying fees, attending ethics training, filing periodic reports, and keeping books open to inspection. Failure to do so could result in felony penalties.

Fully Protected Speech

The CFTC defended the law as a reasonable regulation of a profession that is needed to protect the public, and not as an abridgment of speech. The court disagreed, however, concluding that legitimate regulation of a profession applies to situations in which a speaker exercises judgment on behalf of a particular client with whose circumstances he is directly acquainted. It noted that the plaintiffs published investment advice and even offered specific buy and sell recommendations, but that "their advice and recommendations are identical for every customer and their products are available to all who wish to purchase them." *Id*. at 478. It found that the plaintiffs' calling "is the selling of ideas, not the trading of commodity futures." *Id*. at 479.

Accordingly, the court held that the publications were entitled to full First Amendment immunity and not the less rigorous protection afforded commercial speech. It noted that the publications, and particularly the plaintiffs' Web sites, contained advertisements, but found that the inclusion of such material did not diminish the level of scrutiny to be applied. The court pointed out that the CFTC was seeking to regulate the substance of the publications and not the advertisements. In particular, it concluded that the CFTC was seeking to regulate the plaintiffs' publications "based solely on a fear that someone may publish advice that is fraudulent or misleading, regardless of whether or not the information published actually is fraudulent or misleading." *Id*. at 482. The court held that such a preemptive strike on speech is an impermissible prior restraint in violation of the First Amendment.

— **Robert Corn-Revere**

G. Courts Make It Clear: Food and Drug Administration Is Subject to First Amendment Scrutiny

Free speech advocates won substantial legal victories against the Food and Drug Administration during 1999. In *Washington Legal Foundation v. Friedman*, a federal district court in the District of Columbia struck down a portion of the Food and Drug Administration Modernization Amendments (FDAMA), as well as FDA guidance documents that restricted the right of drug manufacturers to disseminate information concerning off-label drug uses. The D.C. Circuit held, in *Pearson v. Shalala*, that the FDA's regulations limiting the claims of dietary supplement manufacturers violated the First Amendment. And, in *Western States Medical Center v. Shalala*, a Nevada federal district court struck down a provision of FDAMA that prohibited the advertising of certain drugs.

Washington Legal Foundation v. FDA[1]

In a series of decisions issued in 1999, a federal trial court in the District of Columbia granted a major victory for freedom of speech. The case, *Washington Legal Foundation v. Friedman*, involved a First Amendment challenge to the FDA's restrictions on certain forms of legal promotion of unapproved uses of drugs and devices approved by the FDA for other uses. The case began as a suit to enjoin the FDA from enforcing certain "guidance documents," which limited the rights of manufacturers to distribute reprints of medical textbooks and peer-reviewed journal articles. The guidances also limited the rights of pharmaceutical manufacturers to be involved in continuing medical education seminars. However, the case grew into a statutory challenge when Congress amended FDAMA to add Section 401, which codified much of the substance of the challenged guidance documents.

Section 401 of FDAMA addressed independently authored journal articles and reference texts concerning beneficial and legal, but unapproved, uses of FDA-approved drugs. The statute allowed drug manufacturers to disseminate such materials provided the manufacturers fulfilled certain conditions.[2] For example, manufacturers were required to submit to the FDA an advance copy of the material to be distributed, along with any clinical trial information and reports of clinical experience on the off-label use. Also, manufacturers were required to submit a supplemental new drug application for the off-label use, or certify that they would submit the application within a certain time period. 21 U.S.C. Sec. 360aaa.

The FDA's Continuing Medical Education Guidance, which was not superseded by FDAMA Section 401, prohibited drug manufacturers from supporting seminars and similar scientific programs that involved discussions about off-label uses of a company's products or competing products. The one exception to this general prohibition allowed manufacturers to participate, to a limited extent, in programs or symposia created and operated by an independent program provider.

The district court found that the restrictions prohibited speech, and not conduct, stating that "[t]his court is hard pressed to believe that the agency is seriously contending that 'promotion' of an activity is conduct and not speech, or that 'promotion' is entitled to no First Amendment protection." *Washington Legal Foundation v. Friedman*, 13 F. Supp. 2d 51, 59 (D.D.C. 1998). The court also rejected the FDA's assertion that the speech regulated by the guidance documents falls outside of First Amendment protection because of the federal government's extensive power to regulate the pharmaceutical industry. *Id.* at 60.

The court doubted the continuing validity of the argument "that a certain subset of speech may be considered completely outside of the First Amendment framework because the speech occurs in an area of extensive government regulation." *Id.* Additionally, the court relied upon the Supreme Court's opinion in *44 Liquormart, Inc. v. Rhode Island*, 517 U.S. 484 (1996), for the proposition that the government may not restrict speech without offending the First Amendment simply because it regulates the underlying activity. *Washington Legal Foundation*, 13 F. Supp. 2d at 61.

In a subsequent ruling, the court rejected as "preposterous" the FDA's argument that "the act 'affirmatively permits' speech so long as it complies with the requirements of the statute." *Washington Legal Foundation v. Friedman*, 56 F. Supp. 2d 81, 85 (D.D.C. 1999). The court noted that "[t]he First Amendment is premised upon the idea that people do not need the government's permission to engage in truthful, nonmisleading speech about lawful activity." *Id.*

Analyzing the provisions under *Central Hudson Gas & Electric Corp. v. Public Safety Commission*, 447 U.S. 557 (1980), the court found that the speech at issue was neither false nor inherently misleading. The court also rejected the FDA's attempt to distinguish similar speech on the basis of whether a physician or a drug manufacturer was speaking. Relying on the Supreme Court's recent decision in *Greater New Orleans Broadcasting Association v. United States*, 119 S. Ct. 1923 (1999), the court observed that "decisions that select among speakers conveying virtually identical messages are in serious tension with the principles undergirding the First Amendment." *Washington Legal Foundation*, 56 F. Supp. 2d at 85.

Under *Central Hudson's* second prong, the court found that the FDA lacked a substantial interest in ensuring that physicians receive accurate and unbiased information where, as here, the speech in question was truthful and nonmisleading. However, the government did have a substantial interest, as that interest had been expressed by Congress, in encouraging manufacturers to seek FDA approval of off-label uses.

Moving on to the final prongs of *Central Hudson*, the court found that only one of the conditions contained in Section 401 of FDAMA — requiring submission of a supplemental drug application — directly advanced the substantial government interest of encouraging manufacturers to seek FDA approval of off-label uses. However, the court determined that this condition burdened substantially more speech than necessary to advance the government's legitimate interest because it "amount[ed] to a kind of constitutional blackmail — comply with the statute or sacrifice your First Amendment rights." *Id.* at 87.

The FDA has appealed the decision. Oral argument was heard on Jan. 10, 2000.

Pearson v. Shalala

In another important decision, the D.C. Circuit struck down FDA regulations that limited the health claims that dietary supplement manufacturers can lawfully include on their products. *Pearson v. Shalala*, 164 F.3d 650 (D.C. Cir. 1999). Because the FDA lacks the power to regulate the marketing and sale of dietary supplements, the regulations did not purport to regulate in these areas. Instead, they prohibited manufacturers from making health claims about their dietary supplements unless the FDA first determined, "based on the totality of publicly available scientific evidence ... that there is significant scientific agreement among experts qualified by scientific training and experience to evaluate such claims." 21 C.F.R. Sec. 101.14(c) (1998).

The *Pearson* court ruled that the FDA's restriction on commercial speech violated *Central Hudson's* fourth prong because the regulation did not fit reasonably with the FDA's interests. Applying *Central Hudson*, the court ruled that the health claims were not inherently misleading. To reach this conclusion, the court dismissed, as "almost frivolous," the FDA's argument that health claims lacking "significant scientific agreement" were inherently misleading because they made it impossible for consumers to exercise good judgment at the point of sale. *Pearson*, 164 F.3d at 655. However, the FDA's assertion that health claims on dietary supplements could be "at least potentially misleading because the consumer would have difficulty in independently verifying these claims" could be meritorious, the court concluded. *Id.*

Second, the court determined that the FDA's interests in protecting public health and in preventing consumer fraud were substantial. The court nonetheless held that the regulation did not substantially advance the FDA's interest in protecting public health because the FDA "does not assert that appellants' dietary supplements in any fashion threaten consumers' health and safety." *Id.* at 656. However, the court did find that the regulation was reasonably related to the FDA's interest in preventing consumer fraud. *Id.* But the regulations failed under *Central Hudson's* fourth prong because the regulations did not fit reasonably with the FDA's goal of preventing consumer fraud. The court found that the FDA could have used a less burdensome method of requiring dietary supplement manufacturers to label questionable health claims with disclaimers.

Western States Medical Center v. Shalala

In *Western States Medical Center v. Shalala*, 69 F. Supp. 2d 1288 (D. Nev. 1999), a Nevada district court struck down a FDAMA provision that prohibited the advertising of particular compounded drugs. Specifically, the provision substantially limited a pharmacist's ability to produce compounded drugs — *i.e.*, to mix or alter a drug's ingredients to create a medication for the needs of a specific patient — unless the pharmacist satisfied certain conditions. The FDA sought to impose two requirements: (1) a pharmacist must compound the drug product "for an identified individual patient based on the unsolicited receipt of a valid prescription order"; and (2) a pharmacist must not advertise or promote the compounding of any particular drug, class of drug, or type of drug. 21 U.S.C. Sec. 335a(a), (c).

Applying the *Central Hudson* test, the court first concluded that the FDA's "unsupported assertion that the public will be misled into believing, by implication alone, that compounded drugs have passed FDA tests and been approved" did not justify a conclusion that the speech was "inherently misleading." *Western States*, 69 F. Supp. 2d at 1299. To the contrary, "[p]laintiffs seek to provide truthful information about their compounding services." *Id.* However, the possibility that consumers could be misled justified a conclusion that the speech could be potentially misleading. *Id.* at 1300-01.

The court next determined that the FDA's interests in protecting public health and safety and in maintaining the integrity of the drug approval process were substantial. However, it found that the FDA's interest in allowing the availability of compounded drug products, but limiting the scope of compounding, was not substantial. The court so ruled because the FDA has never regulated the production or sale of compounded drug products.

Applying the third prong of *Central Hudson*, the court found that the FDA failed to show the regulation directly advanced either of the government interests asserted. Relying on *Pearson* and *Washington Legal Foundation*, the court held that the regulation did not directly advance the FDA's protection of the public health because "suppression of truthful and accurate information as a means to protect society from its own misuse is anathema to the principles of the First Amendment." *Id.* at 1305. The court further found that the statute did not directly advance the goal of preserving the integrity of the FDA approval process: "If the FDA were concerned with ensuring that drug producers not avoid FDA regulations, it could easily require that all drugs, including compounded drugs, obtain FDA approval before being introduced into the stream of commerce." *Id.* at 1306.

Under the last prong of *Central Hudson*, the court found that the restriction was more extensive than necessary to serve the interests it supported. A proper regulation in this case, the court said, would require a disclaimer as to the evidence that supports the claims, rather than an outright ban of the speech.

*   *   *

These three cases amount to a seismic disruption in the FDA's position vis-a-vis the food and drug industry. The FDA heretofore acted as though the First Amendment did not apply to it — an argument the FDA in fact made in its lower court briefs in the *Washington Legal Foundation* case. The FDA's subjection to the First Amendment will enhance the ability of manufacturers to communicate with, and distribute information to, those who need information most: physicians and their patients.

— Daniel E. Troy

---

[1] The author of this section, Daniel E. Troy, and his law firm, Wiley, Rein & Fielding, represent the Washington Legal Foundation (WLF) in its First Amendment challenge to the FDA.

[2] These uses, known as "off-label uses," are necessary to the practice of medicine simply because medical technology develops faster than the FDA can track it. Thus, it is important for physicians who are making treatment decisions for patients to have the most up-to-date information about all uses of each FDA-approved drug. Off-label uses are especially significant in certain medical fields, such as oncology, where at least five of the most commonly used cancer drugs are used off-label 70 percent of the time. U.S. General Accounting Office, *Off-Label Drugs: Reimbursement Policies Constrain Physicians in Their Choice of Cancer Therapies*, Pub. No. GAO/PEMD-91-14 (1991), at 21-22.

H. High Court Surprise: Limit on Release of Public Records Is Not Speech Restriction

Three laws that discriminate against the commercial usage of public records were struck down by lower federal courts in 1998 and 1999. But the U.S. Supreme Court dealt a surprising blow to commercial speech rights by reversing one federal appeals court decision and vacating another. The Court viewed a California law that allows the release of public records for many noncommercial purposes — but not for commercial uses — as a denial of access rather than a speech restriction.

United Reporting Case

In June 1998, the U.S. Court of Appeals for the Ninth Circuit struck down a California law that prohibited the release of arrestee address information for commercial purposes. *United Reporting Publishing Corp. v. California Highway Patrol*, 146 F.3d 1133 (9th Cir. 1998). The law allowed the release of such information when used for a "scholarly, journalistic, political, or governmental purpose" or for "investigative purposes" by a licensed investigator.

The privately owned United Reporting Publishing Corp. had challenged the law earlier in federal district court, contending the statute violated its First Amendment rights. United Reporting sells the names and addresses of individuals arrested for crimes to attorneys, insurance companies, drug and alcohol counselors, religious counselors, and driving schools.

In November 1996, the district court ruled that the law violated the company's free speech rights. The Los Angeles Police Dept. (LAPD) appealed to the Ninth Circuit, arguing that the law was necessary to protect the privacy rights of arrestees who would be bombarded with solicitations from attorneys and others offering their services.

The Ninth Circuit acknowledged that the government had a substantial interest in protecting the privacy of arrestees. However, the appeals court agreed with the district court that the law violated commercial speech rights because it failed to directly and materially advance the government's interest in protecting that privacy.

According to the court, the "myriad of exceptions" for releasing the information undermined the law's purported purpose in protecting privacy. "Having one's name, crime, and address printed in the local paper is a far greater affront to privacy than receiving a letter from an attorney, substance abuse counselor, or driving school eager to help one overcome his present difficulties," the Ninth Circuit wrote.

U.S. Supreme Court Decision

The Los Angeles Police Dept. appealed the case to the U.S. Supreme Court, which granted *certiorari* in January 1999. *LAPD v. United Reporting Publishing Corp.*, 525 U.S. 1121 (1999).

The LAPD contended the lower courts applied the wrong analysis when they examined the constitutionality of the law as a restriction on commercial speech under *Central Hudson Gas & Electric Corp. v. Public Service Commission*, 447 U.S. 557 (1980). According to the LAPD, the law does not implicate the First Amendment or restrict speech, but instead is "no more than an access restriction." The LAPD claimed that if the High Court struck down the California law it would call into question the constitutionality of 80 other federal and state laws with similar "commercial purpose restrictions."

On Dec. 7, 1999, the Supreme Court ruled 7 to 2 in favor of the law, finding it to be only an access restriction, at least for purposes of United Reporting's facial attack. *LAPD v. United Reporting Publishing Corp.*, 120 S. Ct. 483 (1999). "This is not a case in which the government is prohibiting a speaker from conveying information the speaker already possesses," Justice Rehnquist wrote in his majority opinion.

Justice Rehnquist cited the Court's 1978 decision *Houchins v. KQED, Inc.*, 438 U.S. 1, 14 (1978), for the proposition that neither the First Amendment nor the Fourteenth Amendment mandates a right of access to government information or sources of information within the government's control. The High Court noted that California could decide not to release the information to the public at all.

Justices Ginsburg and Scalia authored concurring opinions. Justice Ginsburg noted that the statute did not prohibit the publication of arrestee address information once it reached the public domain. Justice Scalia wrote separately, finding that if the court examined the law as an as-applied challenge, as opposed to a facial challenge, the law may be analyzed as a speech restriction.

Even the two dissenters, Justices Stevens and Kennedy, agreed with the majority that the California law "is really a restriction on access to government information rather than a direct restriction on protected speech." Justice Stevens determined that, because California was discriminating on who had access to the information "based on its desire to prevent the information from being used for constitutionally protected purposes," it had the burden of justifying its conduct.

California could not meet its burden, Justice Stevens found, because the law clearly fails to advance its purported privacy interests. Because the law allows widespread access to the information, "the State has eviscerated any rational basis for believing that the Amendment will truly protect" privacy rights. Justice Stevens determined that a more likely reason for the law was not an interest in protecting privacy but an interest in preventing lawyers from soliciting law business. "Ultimately, this state interest must fail because at its core it relies on discrimination against disfavored speech," he wrote.

Amelkin v. McClure

United Reporting was not the only case in the federal courts over the release of public records for commercial purposes. The U.S. Court of Appeals for the Sixth Circuit struck down a Kentucky law that prohibited the release of accident reports except to newsgathering organizations for news purposes. *Amelkin v. McClure*, 168 F.3d 893 (6th Cir. 1999).

The Kentucky law generally provided that all accident reports filed with the state police department remain confidential and "exempt from public disclosure." The law made two exceptions: when the material is produced to a "properly executed subpoena" and when the material is "made available to a newsgathering organization, solely for the purpose of publishing or broadcasting the news."

A group of chiropractors, attorneys, and an individual who desires to publish a commercial newspaper containing accident report information challenged the law, contending it violated commercial speech rights.

The state argued, much like the LAPD in *United Reporting*, that the statute is only a "pure denial of access statute" that does not restrict speech. The Sixth Circuit rejected that argument, noting that the statute's specific prohibition against a newsgathering organization using a report for commercial purposes is a content-based restriction.

The Sixth Circuit determined that the law failed the third prong of the *Central Hudson* test — whether the regulation directly and materially advanced the government's interest. The appeals court said the newsgathering exception in the law "precludes the statute from directly and materially advancing the government's purported privacy interest." That exception showed an "overall irrationality" and "renders the statute unconstitutional under the First Amendment," the Sixth Circuit wrote.

The state appealed to the U.S. Supreme Court. On Dec. 13, 1999, the Supreme Court issued a brief order vacating the Sixth Circuit decision and ordering the appeals court to reevaluate the Kentucky law in light of the High Court's decision in *United Reporting*.

Rhode Island Realtors Case

Still another federal court struck down a law that barred the use of public records for commercial purposes in 1999. *Rhode Island Association of Realtors, Inc. v. Whitehouse*, 51 F. Supp. 2d 107 (Dist. R.I. 1999).

The case involved a challenge to a section of a Rhode Island law prohibiting the use of public records "to solicit for a commercial purpose." The Realtors association sought a declaratory judgment against the law, contending it violated the group's commercial speech right to obtain records on recently licensed real estate agents to solicit new members.

The district court judge cited three federal appeals court cases, including the Ninth Circuit's *United Reporting* decision, for the proposition that "attempts to prohibit the use of public records for solicitation purposes consistently have been held to violate First Amendment guarantees."

The state attorney general's office appealed the decision to the U.S. Court of Appeals for the First Circuit. The state contended — as it did before the federal district court judge — that the Realtors association did not have legal standing to seek a declaratory judgment.

In December 1999, in *Rhode Island Association of Realtors, Inc. v. Whitehouse*, 199 F.3d 26 (1st Cir. 1999), the First Circuit affirmed the lower court ruling. The appellate court's opinion is confined to the standing issue; the attorney general did not challenge the district court ruling that the statute was unconstitutional to the extent it "prohibits the use of public information to solicit for commercial purposes."

"We must therefore accept that determination [that the law is unconstitutional] unless we find that the Attorney General is correct in his thesis that the district court should not have heard the case," the First Circuit wrote. The court ruled the association had standing to challenge the statute "because a sufficiently imminent threat of injury loomed."

— **David L. Hudson, Jr.**

I. Ku Klux Klan as Public Radio Underwriter?

National Public Radio stations have become increasingly creative in seeking corporate underwriters in a time of reduced government support. But the general manager of KMWU, an NPR station at the University of Missouri-St. Louis, was not quite prepared for such an offer from the Knights of the Ku Klux Klan, Realm of Missouri. The Klan was apparently seeking to reach a more sophisticated audience, and saw NPR's "All Things Considered" as an ideal medium. Its support would have involved the airing of 15-second spot announcements that recognized, *inter alia*, the Klan's declared mission "to protect the rights of white people."

The station (and the university's chancellor) politely but firmly declined Klan support, expressing their concern about the potential impact of the Klan's message on its other supporters and on the station's capacity to serve a racially diverse student body. The station presumably expected that would be the end of the matter. But the Klan had other plans and soon took the station to federal court, claiming that the station's rebuff curbed its First Amendment right of access to a public forum to express an admittedly unpopular, but nonetheless legally protected, viewpoint.

A U.S. magistrate judge ruled in late 1998 against the Klan's claims and sustained the station's action in *Knights of the Ku Klux Klan v. Bennett*, 29 F. Supp. 2d 576 (E.D. Mo. 1998). That court relied heavily on the recent Supreme Court decision in *Arkansas Educational Television v. Forbes*, 523 U.S. 666 (1998), finding that neither the public radio station nor its corporate sponsorship program could be deemed a public forum for purposes of underwriter access.

Indeed, the most apt description of such a station seemed to be a nonpublic forum, within which editorial judgments about content, including selection of underwriters, remained essentially beyond judicial review. Moreover, the university's decision to refuse Klan sponsorship reflected "business and economic reasons and not [an attempt] ... to suppress [the Klan's] views." Thus the rationale was comparable to the "lack of viewer interest" which in *Forbes* led Arkansas public television to deny air time to marginal congressional candidates.

The case was argued in the U.S. Court of Appeals for the Eighth Circuit in mid-September 1999. The Klan attorney insisted that the station's rebuff entailed forbidden viewpoint suppression. The university, meanwhile, continued to argue that, within a nonpublic forum, such judgments are constitutionally acceptable — at least so long as they are not viewpoint-driven. This appeals court has had more than its share of such cases; *Forbes* went twice through the Eighth Circuit, and was followed closely by a candidate's very similar challenge to the policies of Iowa Public Television.

While nothing else may be quite like Ku Klux Klan sponsorship of "All Things Considered," the medium if not the message is certainly familiar to this particular court. On Feb. 17, 2000, the Eighth Circuit ruled in favor of the station and against the Klan, as had the district court.

— Robert M. O'Neil

J. Federal Appeals Courts Reach Different Rulings on Compelled Ads for Food Producers

Federal laws that compel food producers to contribute to generic advertising programs — and the impact of those laws on commercial speech rights — remained a contentious legal issue in 1999. Federal appeals courts issued divergent rulings on the issue that reached the U.S. Supreme Court in the 1997 case *Glickman v. Wileman Bros. & Elliott, Inc.*, 521 U.S. 457 (1997).

Food producers allege that programs requiring them to fund generic advertising that conflicts with their own messages or says something they don't agree with amount to compelled speech. They cite the fundamental First Amendment principle that the government cannot compel someone to speak or to endorse certain speech. The Court's compelled speech line of cases emerges from challenges involving labor union dues and bar association fees.

Federal and state regulators insist the matter is one of economic regulation, not speech restriction or forced speech. The generic ads simply stimulate interest in a particular product and are part of a broader marketing scheme that benefits the producers, they contend.

In *Wileman* the U.S. Supreme Court agreed with this reasoning. By a 5-to-4 vote the Court upheld a federal program forcing fruit producers to pay for generic ads to promote their industry. The High Court noted that the assessments in the *Wileman* case, mandated by U.S. Department of Agriculture marketing orders, are part of a larger statutory scheme designed to regulate economic products. Essentially, the Court viewed the case as one of economic regulation rather than speech compulsion.

"The fact that an economic regulation may indirectly lead to a reduction in a handler's individual advertising budget does not itself amount to a restriction on speech," Justice Stevens wrote for the majority.

Instead of applying the standard *Central Hudson* test for examining the constitutionality of regulations infringing on commercial speech, the High Court majority ruled there was no First Amendment issue raised by the program. Instead, the majority said it was "simply a question of economic policy for Congress and the Executive to resolve."

Justice Stevens wrote that the marketing orders must not: (1) impose any restraint on the freedom of any producer to communicate any message to any audience; (2) compel any producer to engage in any actual or symbolic speech; or (3) compel the producers to endorse or finance any political or ideological views.

Ninth Circuit Decisions: *Wileman* Controls

In light of the High Court's decision in *Wileman*, the U.S. Court of Appeals for the Ninth Circuit issued rulings in two cases — *Gallo Cattle* and *Cal-Almond* — upholding marketing orders for milk and almond producers respectively.

In *Gallo Cattle Co. v. California Milk Advisory Board*, 185 F.3d 969 (9th Cir. 1999), the operator of a dairy ranch and the state's largest cheese maker challenged the constitutionality of a milk marketing order issued by the California Milk Advisory Board. The order forced Gallo to contribute to generic ads implying that all California cheeses were of a certain quality. However, the Ninth Circuit relied on *Wileman* to hold the milk marketing order constitutional.

The Ninth Circuit reached a similar outcome in *Cal-Almond, Inc. v. U.S. Dept. of Agriculture*, 192 F.3d 1272 (9th Cir. 1999). The case involved a federal marketing order that imposes fees on individual almond handlers to fund generic ads. The Ninth Circuit had ruled in 1993 that the law violated the First Amendment. "The First Amendment right of free speech includes a right not to be compelled to render financial assistance for others' speech," the Ninth Circuit wrote. *Cal-Almond, Inc. v. U.S. Dept. of Agriculture*, 14 F.3d 429 (9th Cir. 1993).

However, the U.S. Supreme Court sent the case back to the Ninth Circuit and ordered it to apply the principles from *Wileman*. As in the *Gallo* case, *Wileman* controlled the Ninth Circuit's analysis. The appeals court noted in its September 1999 opinion that *Wileman* "makes plain that such challenges to the wisdom or effectiveness of a promotional program raise questions of economic policy, rather than questions of constitutional import."

Sixth Circuit: Breaking Away From *Wileman*

In *United Foods, Inc. v. United States*, 197 F.3d 221 (6th Cir. 1999), the U.S. Court of Appeals for the Sixth Circuit ruled unconstitutional portions of the Mushroom Promotion, Research, and Consumer Information Act of 1990 that make it possible to compel individual mushroom producers to fund a nationwide mushroom promotion campaign.

United Foods, Inc. claimed that other mushroom producers were shaping the content of the advertising to United's disadvantage. Though its arguments were similar to those of Gallo Cattle and Cal-Almond, United Foods prevailed before the Sixth Circuit in November 1999.

The Sixth Circuit distinguished *United Foods* by comparing the highly regulated fruit industry in *Wileman* with the "unregulated" nature of the mushroom growing business. The court stated that the context of the mushroom business is entirely different from the "collectivized California tree fruit business" and that "mushrooms are unregulated." The Sixth Circuit noted that "the mushroom market has not been collectivized, exempted from antitrust laws, subjected to a uniform price, or otherwise subsidized through price supports or restrictions on supply." In other words, since mushroom growers are not subject to a government marketing order that prescribes generic advertising as part of an extensive scheme of economic regulation, the speech of mushroom growers cannot be compelled in the same way.

Even though the Sixth Circuit took great pains to distinguish the mushroom industry from the California fruit industry, the court seemed to disagree with the result of *Wileman* as well. For example, the Sixth Circuit described *Wileman* as a "controversial 5-4 opinion." The Sixth Circuit also described the *United Foods* case as one of "compelled, commercial speech" and said this area of the law was governed by an "as yet unsettled set of principles."

— **David L. Hudson, Jr.**

K. Cities Continue To Restrict Outdoor Advertising but Ninth Circuit Strikes Washington State Ban

Localities around the country, including Detroit and Los Angeles, continued to implement restrictions on billboards and other types of outdoor advertising in 1999. Although many of these restrictions have been challenged in the courts, few final decisions were issued in the past year.

Ordinances Enacted or Effective in 1999

In June 1999, the city council of Detroit approved a prohibition on certain advertising within 1,000 feet of child care facilities, juvenile detention facilities, libraries, parks, playgrounds, recreation centers, schools, and youth activity centers. The prohibition exempts signs adjacent to highways for which Michigan requires sign permits and that are regulated by the Michigan Highway Advertising Act.

Los Angeles also passed a city ordinance that bans tobacco and alcohol ads in the windows of stores, signs inside shops that are visible from the street, and billboards within 1,000 feet of any residential zone, commercial planned land use area near residential use areas, school, youth center, church, entertainment complex, or government-operated park. The ban, which effectively excludes the prohibited advertising from 90 percent of the city, would have become effective in August 1999 but for a pending lawsuit brought by a group of grocers, liquor store owners, and national beer and wine makers. A federal trial court denied the city's motion to dismiss the lawsuit in October 1999.

Challenges to Ordinances

In February 1999, Eller Media sought a restraining order to halt implementation of the beverage portion of a Cleveland ordinance, passed in 1998, banning tobacco and alcohol advertisements in publicly visible locations. Such advertisements are permitted only in certain business and industrial areas and in locations visible from the rights-of-way of Interstate highways.

In April 1999, the Michigan Supreme Court, in *City of Rochester Hills v. Schultz*, upheld a

127

zoning ordinance that limits commercial speech based on aesthetic considerations. 592 N.W.2d 69 (Mich. 1999). Specifically, the ordinance allows the operation of a home business on property zoned for residential use unless the activity causes "the erection or maintenance of any signs." *Id*. at 70. The court analyzed the ordinance under the commercial speech test set forth in *Central Hudson Gas & Electric Corp. v. Public Service Commission*, 447 U.S. 557 (1980), as it applies to speech that is lawful and not misleading.

Because the parties stipulated that the government's interest in regulating commercial signs in residential areas is substantial, the court focused on the last two prongs of *Central Hudson*. It ruled that the regulation directly advanced the government's interest in retaining the residential character of neighborhoods within the city. Next it determined that, although the regulation was not "the least restrictive means" of implementing the government's goals, it reasonably fit those goals.

As described in Chapter III A, a number of tobacco companies have challenged an attempt by the Massachusetts attorney general to restrict tobacco advertising. Specifically, the companies are challenging regulations that would ban outdoor advertising of tobacco products near schools and playgrounds and ban advertising for tobacco products near schools if the advertising is inside a retail store but visible from the street. The rules also require that any in-store advertisement be placed at least five feet off the floor.

In November 1999, the U.S. Court of Appeals for the Ninth Circuit struck down a county board of health resolution in Washington State that banned outdoor tobacco advertising. The ruling did not rely on any First Amendment grounds, but instead determined that the resolution was preempted by the Federal Cigarette Labeling and Advertising Act, 15 U.S.C. Sec. 1331 *et seq. Lindsey v. Tacoma-Pierce County Health Department*, 195 F.3d 1065 (9th Cir. 1999). The Ninth Circuit's decision — which may be reconsidered en banc — conflicts with similar decisions made by the Second, Fourth, and Seventh circuits. See *Greater New York Metropolitan Food Council, Inc. v. Guiliani*, 195 F.3d 100 (2d Cir. 1999); *Anheuser-Busch, Inc. v. Schmoke*, 101 F.3d 325 (4th Cir. 1996); and *Federation of Advertising Industry Representatives, Inc. v. City of Chicago*, 189 F.3d 633 (7th Cir. 1999).

— Daniel E. Troy

SECTION IV

LIBEL LAW / TORT ACTIONS / MEDIA RESTRAINTS

LIBEL LAW / TORT ACTIONS / MEDIA RESTRAINTS

The Media Institute and its First Amendment Advisory Council graded the three branches of the federal government and state and local government for their support of the First Amendment regarding the above libel law, tort action, and media restraint issues as follows:

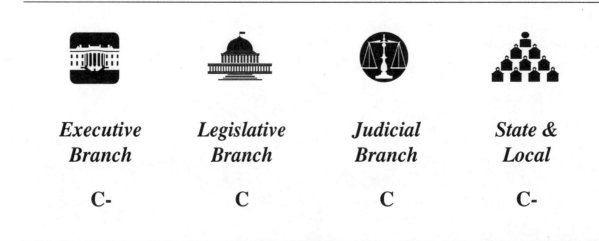

Executive Branch	Legislative Branch	Judicial Branch	State & Local
C-	C	C	C-

A. Liability for Speech Proposing Violence Gains Momentum With Jury Awards

The issue of liability for violent behavior allegedly arising from media presentations continues to be one of the most controversial and fast-developing areas of mass media law.

Portland "Nuremberg Files" Litigation

In February 1999 a federal jury in Portland, Ore., ordered a coalition of abortion protesters to pay $109 million in damages for putting the names and addresses of four doctors on two "wanted"-style posters and a Web site called "The Nuremberg Files." The jury determined that the posters and Web site, although not explicitly threatening, constituted illegal threats of violence under federal clinic-protection and anti-racketeering statutes.

The jury also had before it two posters with a "Deadly Dozen" list, released during a 1995 news conference, which included names and addresses of doctors under the heading "guilty" of "crimes against humanity." A flier resembling an Old West "wanted" poster showed the name, photograph, and home and work addresses of a Missouri abortion provider. None of the actual plaintiffs in the case was a victim of violence as a result of being listed on the posters or Web sites.

The plaintiffs' theory was that the posters and Web sites constituted threats against them. There was evidence presented that three doctors had been killed in recent years after they appeared on "wanted"-style posters. Thus, the plaintiffs argued that when the defendants issued similar posters, the effect was threatening. The trial court had previously rejected a motion for summary judgment. See *Planned Parenthood of the Columbia/Willamette, Inc. v. American Coalition of Life Activists*, 23 F. Supp. 2d 1182 (D. Ore. 1998).

After the verdict, the district judge refused to set aside the jury's award, making detailed findings that the defendants had in fact intentionally engaged in "true threats." The court issued an injunction barring the defendants from any further dissemination of their threatening material. See *Planned Parenthood of the Columbia/Willamette, Inc. v. American Coalition of Life Activists*, 1991 WL 65450 (Feb. 25, 1999); *Planned Parenthood of the Columbia/Willamette, Inc. v.*

American Coalition of Life Activists, 41 F. Supp. 2d 1130 (D. Ore. 1999); Ashbel S. Green, "Jury finds anti-abortion Web site threat to doctors," *Portland Oregonian*, Feb. 3, 1999. An appeal is pending.

"Surprise Television" and the Jenny Jones Case

On May 7, 1999, a Michigan jury awarded $25 million to the family of a gay man murdered by a fellow guest on the "Jenny Jones" television program. The popular nationally syndicated talk program typically features confrontational situations, often in which guests are ambushed with embarrassing personal revelations, such as extramarital affairs.

The lawsuit arose from a Jenny Jones program taped in March 1995 but never aired, except as part of news accounts of the ensuing trials. The show on "secret admirers" featured Scott Amedure, a 32-year-old gay man, who revealed a crush on Jonathan Schmitz, who later said he was heterosexual. Three days after the taping, Schmitz, apparently embarrassed by the revelation, drove to Amedure's home in Oakland County outside Detroit and killed him with a shotgun blast.

Amedure's family later sued Warner Brothers and the show's producer, Telepictures Productions, both owned by Time Warner Inc. The family sought $71.5 million in damages, arguing that the producers were partly to blame for Amedure's death. After seven hours of deliberation, the jury found the show negligent and ordered the companies to pay $5 million for pain and suffering, $20 million for the loss of Amedure's companionship to his family, and $6,500 for funeral expenses.

The defendants had argued that Schmitz agreed to come on the show, even after being told in advance that his secret admirer could be a man or woman. The defendants pointed out that the producers couldn't have known that Schmitz had a history of mental problems, was an alcoholic, and had a thyroid condition, and that any of those factors might have caused him to react violently to Amedure's revelation. The lawyer for the Amedure family countered that the defendants were motivated only by ratings and cared nothing about the guests' welfare, rebuffing the argument that Schmitz might have killed Amedure because the two had had a sexual encounter. An appeal is pending. See Paul Farhi, "'Jenny Jones' show found negligent in murder case," *Washington Post*, May 8, 1999, at A1.

"Natural Born Killers" Litigation

Meanwhile, discovery continued in the so-called "Natural Born Killers" case, *Byers v. Edmondson*. In 1998 the Louisiana Court of Appeal (First Circuit) held that the victims of a convenience store shooting could sue the producers of the film "Natural Born Killers," including Time Warner Entertainment and Oliver Stone, on the grounds that the perpetrators of the shooting had gone on a crime and shooting spree after seeing the film.

The suit alleged that the producers of "Natural Born Killers," labeled collectively in the complaint as "the Hollywood defendants," were liable to the victims for distributing a film "which they knew or should have known would cause and inspire people" to acts of violence by, among other things, "glorifying" such violence and "treating individuals who commit such violence as celebrities and heroes." *Byers v. Edmondson*, 712 So. 2d 681 (1998). Review was denied at the state and U.S. Supreme Court levels, and the case is now proceeding through discovery. See *Byers v. Edmondson*, 726 So. 2d 29 (La. 1998) (denying writ); *Time Warner Entertainment Co., L.P. v. Byers*, 119 S. Ct. 1143 (1999) (denying *certiorari*).

"Hit Man" Case Settles

The *"Hit Man"* litigation ended with a settlement in May 1999. In *Rice v. Paladin Press, Inc.*, 128 F.3d 233 (4th Cir. 1997), *cert. denied*, 118 S. Ct. 1515 (1998), the U.S. Court of Appeals for the Fourth Circuit held that a viable cause of action in tort for aiding and abetting murder existed against the publisher of a murder manual entitled *Hit Man: A Technical Manual for Independent Contractors*. The manual was alleged by the plaintiffs to have been used by a hit man as the blueprint for three contract murders. The publisher had stipulated for the purposes of a motion for summary judgment that it marketed the manual to attract and assist criminals, and that it knew and intended that the manual would be used, upon receipt, by real murderers to plan and execute killings.

The court of appeals held that in these circumstances the First Amendment did not preclude the imposition of liability, and reversed a grant of summary judgment and remanded for trial. The court cited with approval a Justice Department report that argued that the First Amendment did not preclude liability in cases in which a publisher provided detailed information on illegal activity for the purpose of aiding and abetting that activity. See Department of Justice, *Report on the Availability of Bombmaking Information, the Extent to Which Its Dissemination Is Controlled by Federal Law, and the Extent to Which Such Dissemination May Be Subject to Regulation Consistent With the First Amendment to the United States Constitution* (April 1997). The case was settled on the eve of trial, with a cash payment to the families of the murder victims, and an agreement by the defendant to stop marketing the *Hit Man* book.

— **Rodney A. Smolla**

B. Congress Considers Restraints on Violent Media; FTC To Study Entertainment Marketing to Children

A number of legislative and presidential initiatives, introduced in 1999 to curb violence in the media, threaten to restrict the First Amendment rights of advertisers and speakers. None of the legislative measures is likely to pass in 2000 but the president's initiative could lead to advertising restrictions.

S. 1228: Federal Cigarette and Media Violence Labeling and Advertising Act of 1999

On June 16, 1999, Sens. John McCain (R-Ariz.) and Joseph Lieberman (D-Conn.) introduced the Federal Cigarette and Media Violence Labeling and Advertising Act of 1999, S. 1228. This bill would limit the rights of manufacturers and producers of interactive video games, video programs, motion pictures, and sound recordings to advertise their products. Specifically, the bill proposes to amend the Federal Cigarette Labeling and Advertising Act, 15 U.S.C. Sec. 1331 *et seq.*, to require manufacturers to label their products and advertising to inform consumers of the nature, context, intensity of violent content, and age appropriateness of such products.

The mechanics of the bill are relatively simple. The measure would waive antitrust laws and give the industries six months to collaborate on a standardized product labeling system. The Federal Trade Commission would have final authority to modify and approve the system. Once the labeling system was approved, manufacturers would have one year to comply. If manufacturers failed to label their products, the domestic sale or commercial distribution of their products would be banned. Manufacturers and producers who improperly labeled their products would be subject to fines of up to $10,000 per day for every day the product was in the marketplace. Retailers who failed to enforce product age restrictions would be subject to fines of up to $10,000 for each violation of the Act.

The bill was referred to the Senate Commerce Committee. Because Congress did not act on the bill in the first session of the 106th Congress, it is unlikely the legislation will be enacted during the second session. However, there could be hearings on the bill in 2000.

H.R. 2036: Children's Defense Act of 1999

Rep. Henry J. Hyde (R-Ill.) introduced the Children's Defense Act of 1999, H.R. 2036, on June 8, 1999. The most important provisions of the bill involved an amendment to the criminal code, a restriction on sales by music retailers, and a request that the entertainment industry develop voluntary guidelines to decrease negative programming.

Specifically, the bill would have prohibited anyone from knowingly soliciting or exhibiting to a minor "any picture, photograph, drawing, sculpture, video game, motion picture film, or similar visual representation or image, book, pamphlet, magazine, printed matter, or sound recording" that contains sexually explicit or violent material, or detailed verbal descriptions of sexually explicit or violent material, when that material — taken as a whole — predominantly appeals to the prurient interest of minors, is patently offensive to prevailing standards in the adult community, and is utterly without redeeming social importance for minors. H.R. 2036, Sec. 2. The penalty for violating the provision would have been imprisonment.

Additionally, the bill would have required retailers to make available to persons over the age of 18, for on-site review, the lyrics of any sound recording offered for sale. The penalty would have been a fine of $1,000 for each day the retailer failed to make the lyrics available for review.

The bill also would have required the National Institutes of Health (NIH) to conduct a study on the effects of video games and music on child development and youth violence. The measure would have granted temporary antitrust immunity to the entertainment industry to develop voluntary programming guidelines similar to those contained in the television code of the National Association of Broadcasters (NAB).[1] Additionally, the bill would have established a national youth crime prevention demonstration project "to fund intervention models that establish violence-free zones." H.R. 2036, Sec. 6.

The bill was referred to the House Education and the Workforce Committee and the Judiciary Committee on June 8. One month later the bill was referred to the House Education Subcommittee on Early Childhood, Youth, and Families. On June 16, 1999, Rep. Hyde offered this bill as an amendment to H.R. 1501 (discussed below) on the House floor. Prompted by fears that the bill would infringe upon First Amendment freedoms, the left and right joined to defeat the measure by a vote of 282 to 146.

S. 254: Violent and Repeat Juvenile Offender Accountability and Rehabilitation Act of 1999, and H.R. 1501: Consequences for Juvenile Offenders Act of 1999

In May 1999 the Senate passed S. 254, a bill to reduce juvenile crime that Sen. Orrin Hatch (R-Utah) had introduced in January. The House returned the bill to the Senate in July, refusing to consider it on constitutional grounds. In October, the House defeated its own version, H.R. 1501, that Rep. Bill McCollum (R-Fla.) had introduced in April.

Both bills contained a number of provisions to combat juvenile crime, some of which were significant for First Amendment purposes. First, they directed the National Institutes of Health to study the effects of violent video games and music on child development and youth violence. The director of NIH would have been required to coordinate research on youth violence conducted or supported by NIH agencies; identify and develop youth violence research projects; take steps to further cooperation with governmental and nongovernmental agencies; establish a clearinghouse for information about youth violence research; and periodically report to Congress.

Second, like the Children's Defense Act of 1999, the bills proposed to exempt from antitrust laws any joint efforts by the entertainment industry to alleviate the negative impact of violent, sexual, or criminal content on children. They also proposed an antitrust exemption for discussions to promote the telecasting of materials deemed beneficial to the development of children, and discussions regarding the enforcement of voluntary ratings or labeling systems. Third, similar to President Clinton's directive discussed below, the bills instructed the FTC and the attorney general to conduct a joint study of the marketing practices of the motion picture, recording, video, and personal computer game industries.

S. 876: Children's Protection from Violent Programming Act

In April 1999, Sen. Ernest Hollings (D-S.C.) introduced the Children's Protection from Violent Programming Act, S. 876. The bill proposes to amend the Communications Act of 1934 to make it "unlawful for any person to distribute to the public any violent programming during hours when children are reasonably likely to comprise a substantial portion of the audience." S. 876, Sec. 3. The bill would require the Federal Communications Commission to promulgate implementing regulations but would exempt news and sports programming. Premium and pay-per-view cable programming would also be exempt from the FCC's rulemaking. The legislation would require the FCC to immediately revoke the license of any broadcaster who repeatedly violated the Act, and to consider a broadcaster's compliance with the Act as a factor in license renewal.

The measure was referred to the Senate Commerce Committee. The committee held hearings on the bill in May but no legislative action has occurred since then. Therefore, it is unlikely the bill will become law during the 106th Congress.

FTC Study on Marketing of Violent Media to Children

A study requested by the president could lead to advertising restrictions — and raise significant First Amendment concerns. As part of a campaign to address youth violence, on June 1, 1999

President Clinton requested the Federal Trade Commission and the Department of Justice to study the marketing practices of the entertainment industry.

The president asked the agencies to examine: (1) whether the video game, motion picture, and recording industries advertise violent and other material intended for adults in media outlets where children comprise a substantial percentage of the audience; (2) whether these industries use other marketing practices designed to attract children to violent material; (3) whether they have adopted procedures to restrict the sale of adult-rated products to children; and (4) whether these procedures are effective in restricting children's access to adult-oriented material. President Bill Clinton, "Addressing the marketing of violence to children," June 1, 1999 <http://www.whitehouse.gov/ WH/Work/060199.html>.

In response to the president's request, the FTC announced it would study the marketing practices of the entertainment industry to determine whether and to what extent the industry markets adult-rated violent material to children. FTC Chairman Robert Pitofsky emphasized, in a speech to the National Association of Attorneys General, that the primary focus of the study will be on what industry self-regulation is, how it works, and how it can be improved. In addition, the study will examine whether current voluntary restrictions are effective in ensuring that inappropriate products are not sold to children. Finally, the FTC will determine whether advertising for products is more violent than the products themselves.

Criticized for potential agency infringement on the First Amendment, Pitofsky stated: "We understand that this is an area that impacts freedom of expression and that there are appropriate limits on government action imposed by the First Amendment." "FTC chairman outlines agency study on marketing practices of entertainment industry," June 25, 1999 <http://www.ftc.gov/opa/ 1999/9906/violspeech.htm>.

The FTC has already published two notices seeking comment on proposed information requests it plans to send to members of the motion picture, recording, video, personal computer, and coin-operated game industries. Three commenters raised First Amendment concerns: Prof. Erwin Chemerinsky of the University of Southern California, Philip D. Harvey of the Liberty Project, and Prof. Robert M. O'Neil, founding director of the Thomas Jefferson Center for the Protection of Free Expression. Prof. O'Neil suggested that the study "may chill entirely lawful non-deceptive marketing of lawful products — entertainment materials which (unlike most objects of marketing) enjoy First Amendment protection of their own." 64 Fed. Reg. 63,045, 63,046 (1999).

Harvey warned that "although the current proceeding is merely an inquiry, the threat it undoubtedly poses of future governmental restrictions on both commercial and non-commercial speech will not only directly restrain protected commercial speech but also will begin to influence what underlying core expression is produced." *Id.* at 63,046. The FTC dismissed all of these

First Amendment concerns, stating that its purpose is not to enforce existing statutes or regulations but to report its findings to the president, Congress, and the American public. *Id.*

In an act that some have termed "coerced voluntarism," the National Association of Theater Owners agreed to follow the president's request and to enter into a ratings enforcement and educational effort. The effort will require all association members to ask for photo identification when young patrons not accompanied by a parent or guardian seek admission to R-rated films. The association will also begin — in coordination with various churches and civic bodies — a national community education effort to apprise parents of the movie ratings system and the new ID-check policy. President Bill Clinton, "Working to protect youth from movie violence," June 8, 1999 <http://www.whitehouse.gov/WH/Work/060899.html>.

— **Daniel E. Troy**

---

[1] NAB had adhered for many years to a comprehensive voluntary code of conduct, but abandoned these guidelines in 1983 when the Department of Justice challenged them on antitrust grounds.

C. Veggie Libel Laws' Constitutionality Undecided; Fifth Circuit Rules in Favor of Oprah Winfrey

Proponents continue to press for new food disparagement statutes — so-called "veggie libel laws" — though the courts have yet to rule on their constitutionality. Meanwhile, evidence is accumulating that these laws are exerting a chilling effect on protected speech.

Veggie libel laws provide civil or criminal penalties for disparaging statements about food products. Under these laws, disparaging statements can be considered false unless they are supported by "scientific evidence." Further, a general category of product can be disparaged — it need not be a particular brand or producer. Anyone who trades in that product may bring legal action.

Litigation

Many legal experts believe that product disparagement laws violate the First Amendment because they chill speech, but no court has yet ruled on the laws' constitutionality. Four lawsuits involving statutory product disparagement charges have been filed.

The only one that went to trial was *Texas Beef Group (Engler) v. Oprah Winfrey*. In that case, the Texas cattlemen's association sued the popular talk show host after she made comments about hamburger on a show discussing "mad cow disease." The suit was dismissed on Feb. 17, 1998 after a federal district judge ruled that cattle are not perishable agricultural products within the meaning of the Texas law. The plaintiffs appealed the ruling as well as the jury's findings in favor of Winfrey on other counts of the complaint. The U.S. Court of Appeals for the Fifth Circuit heard oral arguments in the case in June 1999 and ruled on Feb. 8, 2000 to uphold the lower court ruling. The court did not rule on the scope of the Texas law but said it was a conventional business defamation case, requiring the cattlemen to show that the statements on the TV show were deliberately reckless or false.

A similar suit against Winfrey and another defendant was filed in Texas state court but was remanded to the federal court, where it awaits disposition.

State Legislative Action

Thirteen states now have food disparagement laws on the books. The law in Colorado is the only one that makes it a crime to disparage food or food products (the others carry civil penalties). Legislatures in Arkansas, Iowa, Maryland, Missouri, New Hampshire, and Vermont have taken up and rejected proposals for veggie libel laws. Similar measures are pending in California and Michigan. A proposal to repeal the Texas law was defeated by a vote of 80 to 57 in 1999.

For the first time since 1990, no food libel laws were introduced during state legislative sessions in 1999. Likewise, no bills have been introduced in the U.S. Congress despite the urgings of some consumer groups.

Impact on Speech

A number of instances where expressive activities apparently have been curtailed by the existence of veggie libel laws were reported by Melody Petersen, writing in the June 1, 1999 issue of the *New York Times* ("Farmers' right to sue grows, raising debate on food safety"):

- Actor Alex Baldwin said that television producers balked at his proposal for a documentary entitled "The History of Food" because a part of the program would have dealt with pesticides, herbicides, and disputed beef-raising practices.
- Robert Hatherill, a research scientist at the University of California at Santa Barbara, said that the publisher of his book, *Eat To Beat Cancer*, cut from his manuscript long passages about growth hormones administered to dairy cattle, and other material that might be targeted under veggie libel laws.
- Vital Health Publishing of Bloomingdale, Ill., called back from the printers a book entitled *Against the Grain: Biotechnology and the Corporate Takeover of Your Food* after receiving a letter from a lawyer for Monsanto Company. The letter stated that Monsanto was concerned that the book might disparage the herbicide sold under the name "Roundup."

The mere existence of food disparagement laws presents a potential for chilling speech, especially when the cost of defending against a lawsuit (or prosecution in Colorado) is taken into account. As of January 2000, for example, the Winfrey case had been in litigation for 44 months and could go on for several more years. Ronald K.L. Collins, director of the FoodSpeak Project at the Center for Science in the Public Interest, points out that the litigation already has accumulated 75 volumes of court records, 5,666 pages of testimony, and millions of dollars in attorneys' fees. "More libel laws: More abridgments of free speech," *Publishers Auxiliary*, April 19, 1999, at 3.

— **Paul K. McMasters**

D. Louisiana Passes Anti-SLAPP Law; Federal, State Courts Take Dim View of SLAPP Suits

The phenomenon known as the Strategic Lawsuit Against Public Participation, or SLAPP suit, was the subject of more legislative and judicial activity in 1999. (The acronym was first coined by Denver professors Penelope Canan and George Pring in two 1988 articles.)

A SLAPP suit is a meritless lawsuit filed to silence or intimidate citizens who exercise their First Amendment rights on matters of public importance. Several states, from California in 1993 to Louisiana in 1999, have passed laws designed to protect individuals from such actions. Meanwhile, the past year witnessed at least two failures by state legislatures to enact anti-SLAPP statutes, but also saw a federal appeals court ruling that could have far-reaching significance for the future of SLAPP suits.

On the Legislative Front

In July 1999, Louisiana became the 14th state to enact an anti-SLAPP law. The measure, modeled after California's anti-SLAPP statute, notes that "there has been a disturbing increase in lawsuits brought primarily to chill the valid exercise of the constitutional rights of speech and petition for redress of grievances." The law provides that SLAPP victims can defend themselves from suits filed to silence free speech and petition rights "in connection with a public issue" by filing a "special motion to strike." The prevailing party on the motion to strike can recover reasonable attorneys' fees and costs.

Anti-SLAPP bills did not fare as well in Oregon and Pennsylvania, where the measures failed to clear their respective state senates. In May 1999 the Oregon House easily passed a bill, which stated that a person "is not civilly liable for speech, influencing action, or otherwise participating in the processes of government, regardless of their intent or purpose." However, in July the Senate weakened the bill and then tabled its own version of the legislation. Jeffrey Lamb, chairman of Oregon Communities for a Voice in Annexation, said the Senate's action would "lead to a lessening of citizen involvement in every public arena." See David Hudson, "Anti-SLAPP bill dies in Oregon Senate," *free! The Freedom Forum Online*, July 9, 1999 <www.freedomforum.org/speech/ 1999/7/9oreslapp.asp>.

A similar fate struck a Pennsylvania anti-SLAPP bill that cleared the Assembly on April 19 by a vote of 198 to 0. The measure would have ensured "that a frivolous lawsuit or a SLAPP can be resolved in a prompt manner by permitting citizens to raise civil immunity to such suits when filing a preliminary objection for legal insufficiency and to obtain a stay of discovery" as provided for in the bill. However, the measure was referred to a Senate committee on environmental resources and energy where it died.

The 14 states with anti-SLAPP statutes are California, Delaware, Georgia, Indiana, Louisiana, Maine, Massachusetts, Minnesota, Nebraska, Nevada, New York, Rhode Island, Tennessee, and Washington.

On the Judicial Front

The U.S. Court of Appeals for the Ninth Circuit ruled in *United States ex rel. Newsham v. Lockheed Missiles & Space Co., Inc.*, 190 F.3d 963 (9th Cir. 1999), that California's anti-SLAPP law could be used in a federal lawsuit to fend off a meritless suit.

The case arose after two individuals filed a claim against Lockheed under the False Claims Act, alleging that the company submitted millions of dollars of false claims for labor on government projects. The company denied the allegations and fired back with several state-law counterclaims, including breach of loyalty, breach of contract, and breach of the implied covenant of good faith.

The federal plaintiffs sought to dismiss the counterclaims as meritless under California's anti-SLAPP law. The California measure, passed in January 1993, allows a party to file a special motion to strike a frivolous lawsuit. The anti-SLAPP statute also allows the recovery of attorneys' fees and costs if the motion to strike is granted.

Lockheed argued that the federal district court was correct in ruling that the California anti-SLAPP law was inapplicable in federal court because it conflicted with certain Federal Rules of Civil Procedure. Lockheed had contended that the Federal Rules already provided provisions for weeding out meritless claims under Rule 8 (requiring specificity in pleadings); Rule 12(f) (motion to strike); Rule 12(b)(6) (motion to dismiss); and Rule 56 (motion for summary judgment).

On appeal the Ninth Circuit reversed, finding that the state anti-SLAPP measure would not result in a "direct collision" with the Federal Rules. The Ninth Circuit recognized that the Federal Rules and the anti-SLAPP law served similar purposes, but added that the anti-SLAPP law "is crafted to serve an interest not directly addressed by the Federal Rules: the protection of the 'constitutional rights of freedom of speech and petition for redress of grievances.'"

The appeals court noted that if the California anti-SLAPP law was held inapplicable in federal court, then litigants might well engage in forum shopping and try to bring lawsuits in federal court rather than state court "Plainly, if the anti-SLAPP provisions are held not to apply in federal court, a litigant interested in bringing meritless SLAPP claims would have a significant incentive to shop for a federal forum," the court wrote.

Another judicial opinion rendered in 1999 shows that courts are increasingly aware of the SLAPP phenomenon, even in states where there is not a specific anti-SLAPP statute on the books.

In *Lobiondo v. Schwartz*, 323 N.J. Super. 391, 733 A.2d 516 (1999), the Superior Court of New Jersey, Appellate Division, issued an opinion highly protective of individuals who exercise their First Amendment rights on matters of public concern. The case involved a defamation action brought by a beach club owner against an octogenarian resident and her three adult daughters who alleged the beach club owner had repeatedly violated local zoning laws. The suit, filed in 1991, eventually resulted in the beach club owner winning jury awards in 1996. But the New Jersey Superior Court reversed on appeal, finding that the plaintiff's original suit was frivolous.

The defendants asked the appellate court to accept the viability of a new tort — called the "SLAPP-back" — that would enable a party to recover compensatory and punitive damages from a party who files a SLAPP suit. The appellate court declined to create a new tort, saying that the "intermediate appellate court should ordinarily defer to the Supreme Court or to the Legislature with respect to the creation of a new cause of action." The New Jersey appeals court said, however, that the defendants could avail themselves of the tort known as malicious use of process. Furthermore, the court wrote that the filing of a SLAPP suit is malicious *per se*.

"We regard the bringing of a suit for the primary purpose of impairing public participation in matters of legitimate public concern and thereby suppressing legitimate public debate and protest as *per se* malicious in this context," the court wrote. "We do not think litigation whose primary intent is to infringe upon another's First Amendment rights can be otherwise regarded."

It remains to be seen whether other states will follow the path of the 14 states and enact specific statutes, or whether the supreme courts of those other states will create the new SLAPP-back tort.

— **David L. Hudson, Jr.**

E. New York Court Thwarts Effort To Expand Libel Law in Celebrity Divorce Case

We have witnessed a series of recent moves to make it easier to impose liability on the media for publishing assertedly false statements. Examples include the proliferation of agricultural disparagement statutes and efforts to redefine California's publicity rights statute in ways that could have opened the door to defamation actions on behalf of "deceased personalities."

This disturbing trend was also evident in a recent New York State appellate court decision in *Huggins v. The Daily News,* which found that newspaper articles about the contentious breakup of a celebrity marriage were not of legitimate public concern. Accordingly, the court held that if the articles were proved false, the plaintiff need only show that the *Daily News* was negligent, not grossly irresponsible, in publishing them

The action was brought by Charles Huggins, ex-husband of singer Melba Moore, against the *Daily News* and reporter Linda Stasi. The suit arose out of three articles about their divorce that appeared in Stasi's "Hot Copy" column. The articles described an out-of-state *ex parte* divorce obtained by Huggins and a number of other legal disputes he had with Moore. The articles reported Moore's claims that her name had been forged on divorce documents, that her assets had been misappropriated, and that she had suffered verbal and physical abuse. Huggins alleged that 18 statements in the *Daily News* articles were defamatory. The New York State Supreme Court dismissed all of the claims on the grounds that the challenged statements were protected opinion.

On April 13, 1999 the Appellate Division, First Department, reversed in an opinion with deeply troubling implications for the media. In reversing, the Appellate Division held that a number of the statements concerning the plaintiff were factual and defamatory, that the plaintiff was a private figure, and — most disturbingly — that the subject matter of the articles involved "quintessentially private matters" that were not "arguably within the sphere of legitimate public concern" within the meaning of *Chapadeau v. Utica Observer-Dispatch,* 38 N.Y.2d 196 (1975). The impact of this last ruling by the Appellate Division was to reduce the plaintiff's burden under New York law to a showing of simple negligence on the part of the paper, instead of the more press-protective standard of "gross irresponsibility" articulated in *Chapadeau* to establish liability (in the event falsity is proved as to one or more of the actionable statements).

New Standard of Newsworthiness?

The New York Court of Appeals had never found an allegedly defamatory publication to fall outside the ambit of the *Chapadeau* standard, and has, in fact, held that the media's judgment is entitled great deference regarding what is newsworthy. Nonetheless, the Appellate Division appeared to create a *per se* rule that matrimonial matters involving a private figure are not newsworthy. It thus rendered a great deal of what has become mainstream news reporting potentially subject to liability under a fault standard that is, in theory, much easier for plaintiffs to meet than the *Chapadeau* standard.

The *Daily News* petitioned for further review by the court of appeals; that petition was granted on June 22, 1999. Oral argument took place on Nov. 17, 1999. An *amicus* brief supporting the *Daily News* filed by a number of First Amendment and media organizations (including the Association of American Publishers) pointed out one consequence of the ruling: that "news editors will no longer be able to rely solely on their editorial judgment in deciding whether to publish an article about a private citizen…. This chilling effect will be compounded so long as there is no clear guidance as to when a news report will be considered to be outside the sphere of public concern."

The New York Court of Appeals handed down its decision on Dec. 20, 1999, unanimously repudiating the Appellate Division ruling. The court reiterated its position that "[a]bsent clear abuse, the courts will not second-guess editorial decisions as to what constitutes matters of genuine public concern." The court held that "[m]anifestly, what Stasi identified as the 'important social issue' of 'economic spousal abuse' was at least arguably within the sphere of legitimate public concern, triggering the *Chapadeau* standard of journalistic fault…. In ruling to the contrary, the Appellate Division did not accord the deference to editorial judgment our decisions require."

—Judith Platt

F. Supreme Court Decision Deals Major Blow to Reporters' 'Media Ride-Alongs' With Police

The U.S. Supreme Court has dealt a major blow to the ability of journalists to engage in the long-standing practice of "media ride-alongs." The Court ruled that the presence of reporters and/or photographers during the execution of a search warrant by government officials violates the Fourth Amendment to the U.S. Constitution. *Wilson v. Layne*, 119 S. Ct. 1692 (1999).

The Supreme Court combined two different cases for oral argument. The first, *Wilson v. Layne*, began in April 1992 when a team of U.S. deputy marshals and county police from Montgomery County, Md., executed a search warrant to arrest Dominic Wilson. Wilson was charged with violating his probation on previous felony convictions, including robbery, theft, and assault with intent to rob. The warrants allowed "any duly authorized peace officer" to arrest Wilson and bring him before the Circuit Court of Montgomery County; there was no mention of any media presence or assistance in the warrants.

An error in a police computer gave rise to the lawsuit. The computer mistakenly listed Wilson's address as the address of his parents. The officers went to his parents' house, accompanied by a reporter and photographer from the *Washington Post*, who were invited by the deputy marshals as part of the U.S. Marshals Service ride-along policy. The officers entered the home and awakened the Wilsons, who were still in their nightclothes. By the time the officers realized that Dominic Wilson was not in the house, the photographer had already taken numerous pictures and the reporter had observed a confrontation between Dominic Wilson's father and the police. Neither representative of the *Washington Post* was involved in the execution of the warrant, nor were any of the photographs published in the newspaper.

The Wilsons sued law enforcement officials in their personal capacities for money damages, contending that the presence of the news media violated their Fourth Amendment right to be free from unreasonable search and seizure. The law enforcement officials argued that they had qualified immunity from suit. The U.S. District Court for the District of Maryland disagreed, denying the officers' motion for summary judgment.

The U.S. Court of Appeals for the Fourth Circuit reversed. *Wilson v. Layne*, 141 F.3d 111

(4th Cir. 1998). The court of appeals held that the officers were entitled to qualified immunity, though it did not rule on whether the actions of the police violated the Fourth Amendment.

The second case involved a warrant executed on a ranch in Montana. In 1993 a magistrate judge issued a warrant authorizing a search of the ranch owned by Paul and Erma Berger for evidence of "the taking of wildlife in violation of Federal laws." One week later, agents from the U.S. Fish and Wildlife Service executed the warrant, accompanied by camera crews from CNN. The Bergers sued the agents for money damages, alleging (as had the Wilsons) that the presence of the media violated their Fourth Amendment rights. The U.S. District Court for the District of Montana disagreed and entered summary judgment in favor of the defendants. *Berger v. Hanlon*, 1996 WL 376634 (D. Mont. 1996).

The U.S. Court of Appeals for the Ninth Circuit reversed. *Berger v. Hanlon*, 129 F.3d 505 (9th Cir. 1997). The circuit split created between the Fourth and Ninth Circuits provided the impetus for the Supreme Court to take the case.

Fourth Amendment Issue

The Court first reviewed the rules regarding qualified immunity. It stated that the proper inquiry for determining whether an official is entitled to qualified immunity entails "first determin[ing] whether the plaintiff has alleged the deprivation of a constitutional right at all, and, if so, proceed[ing] to determine whether that right was clearly established at the time of the alleged violation." *Wilson*, 119 S. Ct. at 1697 (citing *Conn v. Gabbert*, 526 U.S. ___, ___ (1999) (slip op. at 4).

The inquiry thus turned to the Fourth Amendment question. The Court noted that the Fourth Amendment protects the right of the people to be secure in their persons, houses, papers, and effects, with physical entry of the home being the foremost evil against which citizens are to be protected.

The fact that the officers in these cases possessed valid search warrants did not mean that the officers were entitled to bring a newspaper reporter and photographer with them. The Fourth Amendment requires that police actions in execution of a warrant be related to the objectives of that warrant. The Court found that the presence of reporters did not further the objectives of these warrants: "Respondents concede that the reporters did not engage in the execution of the warrant, and did not assist the police in their task. The reporters therefore were not present for any reason related to the justification for police entry into the home...." *Wilson*, 119 S. Ct. at 1698.

The law enforcement officers argued that the presence of the reporters nonetheless served a number of legitimate law enforcement purposes whose effect was more generally felt than executing this specific warrant. The Court rejected each of these in turn.

First, the officers argued that law enforcement personnel should be able to exercise reasonable discretion about whether their law enforcement mission is furthered by the presence of the news media. The Court disagreed, indicating that this argument ignored the important right of residential privacy at the heart of the Fourth Amendment: "It may well be that media ride-alongs further the law enforcement objectives of the police in a general sense, but that is not the same as furthering the purposes of the search. Were such generalized 'law enforcement objectives' themselves sufficient to trump the Fourth Amendment, the protections guaranteed by that Amendment's text would be significantly watered down." *Id.*

Second, the officers argued that the presence of third parties publicized the government's efforts in fighting crime and facilitated the accurate reporting of law enforcement activities. While the Court agreed that its First Amendment precedents give some importance to the press's role in informing the public about the government's crime fighting efforts, it believed that this goal was outweighed by the Fourth Amendment in protecting the privacy of citizens. As the Court stated, "[s]urely the possibility of good public relations for the police is not enough, standing alone, to justify the ride-along intrusion into a private home." *Id.*

Finally, the officers argued that the presence of third parties could serve to minimize police abuses and could also protect the safety of police officers. Again, the Court agreed in principle that some benefit along these lines might be derived from media ride-alongs. However, it found that in the present cases the record was significantly different. The reporters were working on a story for their own purposes, and their presence was not intended to, nor did it in fact, protect the officers.

Qualified Immunity

Despite finding a Fourth Amendment violation, the Court held that the officers had a qualified immunity preventing them from being liable for damages in these cases. Whether a qualified immunity exists turns on whether it was objectively reasonable, at the time of the action, to determine whether legal rules were being broken. The Court held that it was not unreasonable at the time either warrant was executed for a police officer to believe that bringing media observers along during the execution of the warrant was lawful. The constitutional question in the case was by no means open and shut. Media ride-alongs were a common police practice at the time, with no judicial opinions holding that the practice was unlawful once the officers entered a private home. Thus, "given such an undeveloped state of the law, the officers in this case cannot 'have been expected to predict the future course of constitutional law.'" *Id.* at 1701 (citing *Procunier v. Navarette*, 434 U.S. 555, 562 (1978)).

It is interesting to note that while the Court found a Fourth Amendment violation to exist, it did not decide whether the exclusionary rule would apply to any evidence discovered or developed by the media representatives to prevent that evidence from being introduced at trial. This is because it was the presence of the media, not the presence of the police, in the home that created the Fourth Amendment violation.

On remand to the U.S. Court of Appeals for the Ninth Circuit, that court reversed the grant of summary judgment to the news media in *Berger v. Hanlon.* The Ninth Circuit noted that the Supreme Court had recently ruled that the law enforcement officers and the news media were entitled to qualified immunity. However, the appeals court declared that the media defendants did not, and were not entitled to, assert a claim of qualified immunity and were not entitled to receive summary judgment in their favor on that issue.

— **Richard M. Schmidt, Jr. and Kevin M. Goldberg**

C-

G. California Employee Privacy Ruling Against ABC Endangers Undercover Reporting

An opinion on employee privacy by the California Supreme Court extends a trend endangering undercover investigative journalism. The court ruled that employees working in an office to which the general public does not have unfettered access enjoy a limited expectation that their conversations and other interactions will not be secretly videotaped by undercover television reporters, even if those conversations may not be completely private from the participants' co-workers. The case, involving an ABC story on a business providing psychic readings via telephone, is *Sanders v. ABC*, 978 P.2d 67 (1999).

In 1992, ABC reporter Stacy Lescht obtained a job as a "telepsychic" at Psychic Marketing Group (PMG). Like other telepsychics employed in PMG's Los Angeles office, Lescht gave "readings" to customers who telephoned PMG's 900 number. She worked with other telepsychics in a large room with rows of cubicles. Each cubicle was enclosed on three sides by five-foot high partitions. In all, up to 100 telepsychics could be working at any given time. The PMG facility was unlocked during business hours but PMG, by internal policy, prohibited access to the office by nonemployees without specific permission.

Lescht engaged in conversations with other telepsychics, which she taped using a "hat cam" — a small camera hidden inside her hat; she used a microphone attached to her brassiere to record sound. She recorded several conversations with her co-workers, and in particular recorded two conversations with a co-worker named Mark Sanders. During the first conversation, a third employee was standing just outside Lescht's cubicle. The conversation was held in a moderate tone of voice; a fourth employee, who was passing by at the time, overheard the conversation and joined in.

The second conversation took place in Sanders's cubicle. It was conducted in a softer tone of voice. The conversation was interrupted briefly when Sanders received a customer call and again when a passing co-worker offered the two a snack. During this conversation, Sanders discussed his personal aspirations and beliefs with Lescht and offered her a psychic reading.

153

Causes of Action

ABC's "PrimeTime Live" broadcast a story about the telepsychic industry that included a short excerpt from the second Sanders-Lescht conversation. Sanders pled causes of action based upon this broadcast, but all were disposed of without trial. However, he also pled two causes of action based solely upon the videotaping: (1) violation of California Penal Code Section 632, which prohibits the nonconsensual recording of a confidential communication, defined as one made in circumstances in which the parties may reasonably expect that the conversation may not be overheard or recorded; and (2) common law invasion of privacy.

In a special verdict form, the trial court jury was asked whether the conversation upon which Lescht allegedly intruded was conducted "in circumstances in which the parties may reasonably have expected that the communications may have been overheard." The jury answered "yes" to this question; the trial court then ordered judgment in favor of the defendants on the Section 632 cause of action.

The defendants then moved to dismiss the remaining cause of action for invasion of privacy. The court denied this motion, allowing the trial to go forward on the issue of liability for photographic intrusion. The trial court ruled that Sanders had a limited right of privacy against being secretly videotaped in his workplace, even if his conversations could have been overheard by co-workers. The trial court jury ruled in favor of Sanders, awarding him $335,000 in compensatory damages and $300,000 in punitive damages.

The California Court of Appeal reversed the judgment entered for the plaintiff and entered a judgment in favor of the defendants instead. The court held that the invasion of privacy tort requires an invasion into a secluded area where one has an objectively reasonable expectation of privacy and confidentiality.

Petition for Review Granted

The California Supreme Court granted the plaintiff's Petition for Review. It limited the issues to be briefed and argued to the following:

- whether a person who lacks a reasonable expectation of complete privacy in a conversation because it could be seen and overheard by co-workers (but not the general public) may nevertheless have a claim for invasion of privacy intrusion based upon a television reporter's covert videotaping of that conversation;
- whether the jury's findings in the first phase of the trial, on liability under Section 632, legally precluded maintenance of a common law intrusion claim; and
- whether the jury instructions in the second phase of trial, on liability for intrusion, were prejudicially erroneous.

The California Supreme Court ruled for the plaintiff on all of these questions.

The California Supreme Court began its consideration of the first issue by reviewing its recent decision in *Shulman v. Group W Productions, Inc.*, 18 Cal. 4th 200 (1998), which had not been decided when either the trial court or the court of appeal issued its ruling. In *Shulman*, the California Supreme Court had defined the tort of intrusion as having two elements: (1) intrusion into a private conversation, place, or matter; (2) in a manner highly offensive to a reasonable person. *Id.* at 231.

Elaborating on the first element, the court noted that an expectation of privacy, in order to be reasonable, need not consist of complete or absolute privacy. In *Shulman*, the plaintiff was a severely injured accident victim who was taped having a conversation with rescue personnel in a medivac helicopter. The record was unclear whether other members of the general public were present or could overhear the conversations between the plaintiff and the rescue personnel. However, as *Shulman* and other cases have pointed out, "a person may reasonably expect privacy against the electronic recording of a communication even though he or she had no reasonable expectation as to confidentiality of the communication's contents." *Sanders*, 978 P.2d at 72.

Rather, the California Supreme Court noted, "there are degrees and nuances to societal recognition of our expectations of privacy: the fact the privacy one expects in a given setting is not complete or absolute does not render the expectation unreasonable as a matter of law." *Id.* The California Supreme Court concluded that the reasonableness of a person's expectation of visual and aural privacy depends on three things: (1) who might have been able to observe the interaction; (2) the identity of the claimed intruder; and (3) the means of the intrusion.

The defendants had argued that a doctrine of *per se* workplace privacy would dangerously chill investigative journalism. The California Supreme Court claimed that it had not adopted a *per se* doctrine, holding only that the possibility of being overheard by co-workers does not, as a matter of law, render unreasonable an employee's expectations that his or her conversations with co-workers will not be secretly videotaped.

This is where the second element of the tort, relating to offensiveness, came into play: "Nothing we say here prevents a media defendant from attempting to show, in order to negate the offensiveness element of the intrusion tort, that the claimed intrusion, even if it infringed on a reasonable expectation of privacy, was 'justified by the legitimate motive of gathering the news.'" *Id.* at 77 (citing *Shulman*, 18 Cal. 4th at 236-37).

The California Supreme Court then addressed whether the common law claim of intrusion was negated by the finding of the trial court jury: that the communications were made in a situation in which Sanders could reasonably expect to have been overheard, and that this negated any claim for common law intrusion. The defendants contended, and the court of appeal had agreed, that the jury had determined that Sanders had no reasonable expectation of privacy in the conversations.

The California Supreme Court disagreed: "There was no evidence the public was invited into the PMG Los Angeles office, or that the office was visited by the press or other public observers on a regular basis, or was ordinarily subject to videotaped surveillance by the mass media." *Sanders*, 978 P.2d at 78. The California Supreme Court noted — as it had in answering the first question — that the fact that co-workers may have overheard a workplace conversation does not as a matter of law eliminate all expectations of privacy the participants may have.

Jury Instructions

Finally, the California Supreme Court ruled that certain jury instructions given during the second phase of trial, relating to the elements of intrusion, were not prejudicially erroneous. The defendants complained that the phrase "solitude or seclusion" was omitted from the following instruction:

> The essential elements of an intrusion claim are, one, the defendant intentionally intruded physically or otherwise upon the [solitude or seclusion,] private affairs or other concerns of the plaintiffs by photographing plaintiffs with hat cams, and two, the intrusion was substantial and of a kind that would be highly offensive to an ordinary reasonable person.

The Supreme Court noted that it had used that instruction in the past but it is not a unique or essential label for a reasonable expectation of privacy.

The defendants also argued that two other jury instructions generally abandoned the requirement of a reasonable expectation of privacy by substituting for it the expectation of not being surreptitiously photographed. The instructions at issue read as follows:

> (2) The tort of invasion of privacy includes intrusions by clandestine photography of a person in his workplace if photographs are secretly taken of plaintiff without his or her consent in circumstances where a reasonable person would reasonably expect that the particular defendant would be excluded; and

> (3) Employees take the risk that others present may not be what they seem to be, and that what is heard and seen at a workplace may be repeated outside the workplace. But employees in a workplace not open to the public do not necessarily take the risk that what is heard and seen will be transmitted by photography to the public at large.

The Supreme Court also rejected these arguments. It noted that the reasonableness of a privacy expectation must have some context and must be referenced in relation to the identity of the intrusion and the nature of the intruder. As such, it was proper for the jury to consider whether the plaintiff could reasonably expect that he would not be secretly videotaped in his workplace by a representative of the mass media.

The judgment of the court of appeal was reversed and the case was remanded to that court for further proceedings consistent with the California Supreme Court's opinion.

— Richard M. Schmidt, Jr. and Kevin M. Goldberg

H. Sixth Circuit Ruling on Kentucky State Publications Weakens Free Speech Rights of College Journalists

The free speech rights of college newspapers and other on-campus publications are on shaky ground after a decision by the U.S. Court of Appeals for the Sixth Circuit. The court upheld a ban on distribution of the Kentucky State University student yearbook and allowed school administrators to influence the content of the school newspaper.

The case is *Kincaid v. Gibson*, 1999 U.S. App. LEXIS 21385 (6th Cir. 1999). This case marks the first time that the landmark Supreme Court decision in *Hazelwood School District v. Kuhlmeier*, 484 U.S. 260 (1988), has been used to restrict the free speech rights of the college press.

Background

Kentucky State University (KSU) is a state-funded public university. It publishes a student newspaper called the *Thorobred News* and a biennial yearbook called *The Thorobred*. Both are operated on KSU property and are funded by the university, though the yearbook is funded at least partially through a mandatory $80 student activities fee. Both publications are subject to oversight by KSU's Student Publications Board, which includes both students and university administrators.

As of 1994, the Student Publications Board had not yet adopted a governing policy detailing the scope of its oversight of student publications. However, the KSU student handbook contained a section entitled "Student Publications," which outlined the mission of these publications and the limits on their autonomy.

The Student Publications Board was given expansive review powers over the *Thorobred News* and *The Thorobred*. Among the Board's stated duties were:

> 1. Approve the written publications policy of each student publication, including such items as purpose, size, quantity controls, and time, place, and manner of distribution;

2. Set qualifications for and (upon nominations by the Student Publications Advisor), appoint the editor of each publication who shall serve for a one-year term, unless reappointed or removed by the Board for cause;

3. Set qualifications for and appoint staff members for each publication upon nomination of its editor with concurrence of the Student Publications Advisor, also, remove any of these staff members for cause. *Kincaid*, 1999 U.S. App. LEXIS 21385 at 4.

The Board was also expected to ensure that the *Thorobred News* maintained at least two standards of quality control:

- Report accurately and fairly newsworthy campus events.
- Pursue important news events to make sure they are reported upon and commented upon in the editorial pages with comprehension and full understanding of the facts. *Id.*

Plaintiff Capri Coffer was the editor in charge of the 1992-94 yearbook. She selected the theme "Kentucky State: Destination Unknown" for the yearbook, choosing to include photographs depicting the goings-on at the KSU campus as well as current events in the community and the world at large. She chose a purple cover for the yearbook, rather than the university colors of gold and green, though this was not the first time that the gold and green colors were not used.

When final copies of the yearbook were delivered to KSU, defendant Betty Gibson, then the vice president for student affairs, was not impressed by Coffer's efforts. She disliked the purple cover and called the theme and title vague. She also disagreed with the inclusion of pictures of current events and public figures unrelated to KSU, claiming the yearbook contained a paucity of school-related figures and events. Finally, she complained that many of the pictures lacked captions. After consulting with the university president, Gibson instructed the director of student life to confiscate every copy of the yearbook with the intent to destroy them.

At the same time, Gibson was wielding a heavy hand over the *Thorobred News*. According to the plaintiffs, certain comic strips were dropped from the paper after Gibson had criticized the strips for making fun of the administration. The plaintiffs also alleged that Gibson directed the newspaper's publications coordinator, a faculty member named Laura Cullen, to prohibit the *Thorobred News* from publishing a certain letter to the editor and to convince the students to publish more positive news in the paper.

Cullen refused. She was then transferred to a new position in the university housing office without benefit of notice or hearing, though she was reinstated as publications coordinator one month later after protesting her transfer through the proper KSU grievance procedure. At the time of her reinstatement, Cullen was given a number of specific directives as to how she was to oversee the publication of the *Thorobred News*.

District Court Suit

Coffer and fellow student Charles Kincaid, a member of the newspaper staff, filed suit against Gibson and other university administrators in the U.S. District Court for the Eastern District of Kentucky, on behalf of a proposed class of students. The suit claimed that pursuant to 42 U.S.C. Sec. 1983, Gibson's interference with the newspaper and her refusal to distribute the yearbook constituted a violation of their First Amendment rights to free speech and free association.

The suit also claimed that the confiscation of the yearbook was an unlawful taking of the students' property under the Fourteenth Amendment and a breach of the school's contractual duty to provide students with a yearbook in return for their $80 student activities fee. Finally, the plaintiffs alleged that the defendants had engaged in an arbitrary government action in violation of Section 2 of the Kentucky Constitution. The suit sought both damages and injunctive relief.

The defendants moved to dismiss the First Amendment claims, the breach of contract and deprivation of property claims, and all claims against the school officials in their official capacity. On June 26, 1996, the district court granted this motion in part. Citing the Eleventh Amendment to the U.S. Constitution, the district court dismissed all claims for monetary damages against the defendants in their official capacities. It also dismissed the claim that the failure to distribute the yearbooks constituted a deprivation of a vested property right under the Fourteenth Amendment. Without elaboration, the court dismissed the claim that the students' right to free association under the First Amendment had been violated. Finally, the district court declined to certify the proposed class of students for class action purposes. The court did, however, let the First Amendment free speech claim, the breach of contract claim, and the claim based upon Section 2 of the Kentucky State Constitution go forward.

The parties then filed cross-motions for summary judgment. On Nov. 14, 1997, the district court granted summary judgment in favor of the defendants. It held that the plaintiffs did not have standing sufficient to claim their First Amendment rights had been violated with regard to the *Thorobred News*, since only a faculty member had been injured in fact. With regard to the school yearbook, the district court held that *The Thorobred* was a nonpublic forum; thus, KSU administrators could, and did, engage in a reasonable amount of discretion in confiscating the yearbook.

On the breach of contract claim, the district court held that the defendants did not act in their individual capacity, but rather in their official capacity. Therefore, they could not be held liable for breach of contract, as the breach of contract claim was for monetary damages and the defendants were entitled to sovereign immunity under the Eleventh Amendment. Finally, there was no violation of Section 2 of the Kentucky Constitution because the defendants had the right to exercise reasonable control over the yearbook and did not act arbitrarily or capriciously in this regard.

Appeal to Sixth Circuit

The students appealed to the U.S. Court of Appeals for the Sixth Circuit. The basis for the appeal was the First Amendment claim that the students' free speech rights were violated through the refusal to distribute the yearbook and the administration's attempts to control the content of the *Thorobred News*. The court of appeals upheld the district court on both counts. *Kincaid v. Gibson*, 1999 U.S. App. LEXIS 21385 (6th Cir. 1999).

The court of appeals first discussed the claim relating to the student yearbook. It reviewed the recent history of the college press in the courts, noting that "in virtually all of these cases, the courts held that the protections afforded by the First Amendment reached 'beyond the schoolyard gates' to protect college newspapers." *Id*. at 15. But the court of appeals also recognized that this protection is not without limit and that the U.S. Supreme Court, in *Hazelwood*, created a test for determining the level of protection afforded a student publication. Despite the fact that *Hazelwood* involved a high school newspaper, and that the *Hazelwood* test had never been applied to a college publication, the court of appeals stated that it would be the governing test in this case.

In *Hazelwood*, the Supreme Court reasoned that a court must first assess the nature of the student's forum in examining the propriety of school officials' conduct with regard to a student. The first element of this inquiry is the intent of the school in chartering the publication. If the school gave students full reign over the publication's content, then the publication was most likely intended to be a public forum; in such a case the school's supervision would be limited to time, place, and manner regulation. If the school did not create a public forum, then school officials may impose any reasonable, non-viewpoint-based restrictions on student speech contained in the publication.

In *Hazelwood*, the Supreme Court concluded that the high school newspaper at issue was not a public forum. The Court cited the following evidence:

> (1) The newspaper was officially sponsored by the school as part of the journalism curriculum and was published as part of the journalism class; (2) the newspaper was under the direct and absolute editorial control of the journalism teacher who selected the paper's editors, set publication dates, assigned stories, advised in

the development of stories, edited, participated in the selection of articles for publication, and negotiated with printers; (3) students received class credit and grades for their roles in publishing the paper; and (4) the school principal conducted a final review of each issue of the publication prior to printing. *Kincaid,* 1999 U.S. App. LEXIS 21385 at 19 (citing *Hazelwood,* 484 U.S. at 268-69).

The court of appeals distinguished *The Thorobred* from the student publication in *Hazelwood.* First, the yearbook was not a product of the classroom or any specific journalism course. Nor did the Student Publications Board intervene in the yearbook's day-to-day operations. Thus, KSU did not exercise the same degree of control over *The Thorobred* as did the officials in *Hazelwood.*

However, the Supreme Court still concluded that *The Thorobred* was a nonpublic forum. The KSU student handbook explicitly stated that the *Thorobred News* and *The Thorobred* were under the management of the Student Publications Board. That handbook also offered several details regarding the Board's role in the publications, including written approval of the publications policy, appointment of editors and the ability to remove them for cause, and the requirement that the staffs use an experienced advisor who may require changes in the form or manner of the publications. Finally, the handbook declared that KSU did not consider the *Thorobred News* to be an official organ of the university.

Because neither publication was a public forum, the court of appeals held that the defendants were entitled to regulate the contents of the yearbook in a reasonable manner. It upheld the district court's conclusion that the defendants' confiscation of the yearbook was reasonable in light of KSU's desire to maintain a favorable image to students, alumni, and the general public.

The court of appeals then addressed the appeal of the district court's ruling that the students lacked standing to challenge Gibson's attempts to control the content of the *Thorobred News.* The district court found that the students had not demonstrated any injury-in-fact, as neither the transfer of Laura Cullen or the "bald allegations" that Gibson's criticism effected censorship of the publication amounted to a "claim of specific present objective harm or a threat of future specific harm." *Kincaid,* 1999 U.S. App. LEXIS 21385 at 25. The court of appeals summarily upheld the district court's ruling.

After the court of appeals issued its opinion, the plaintiffs petitioned the court for rehearing en banc. The court of appeals granted the petition and will rehear the case in early 2000.

— **Richard M. Schmidt, Jr. and Kevin M. Goldberg**

I. Police Seize Journalists' Photographs To Post on 'Name That Suspect' Web Sites

In at least two cases in 1999, law enforcement officials either seized negatives from a photojournalist or simply downloaded photographs from newspaper Web sites without authorization to post those photos on their own sites. These police Web sites were created to permit members of the public to identify potential suspects from riots in East Lansing, Mich., and the Woodstock concert in New York.

Photojournalists and the Associated Press objected to this practice on First Amendment and copyright infringement grounds, but the reaction from law enforcement was one of outright enthusiasm for the efficiency of this identification method. In the case of Lansing, the photographs remain posted; in the case of Woodstock, the photographs have been removed from the Web site. The courts in Michigan did, however, quash some subpoenas against the press on procedural grounds.

East Lansing, Mich.

The issue first arose in this college town. On March 27, 1999, a neighborhood adjacent to the Michigan State University campus erupted into rioting after Duke University defeated MSU in the NCAA Final Four basketball tournament. The riot caused a reported $160,000 in damage, and was a serious public relations setback for East Lansing because the city had been the site of student riots a year earlier when police announced restrictions on drinking at football games.

David McCreery, a free-lance photographer for the Associated Press, captured the riot on film. He sent his negatives to the AP, which put several photographs on the wire. On March 31, McCreery's 21st birthday, he took the negatives to a one-hour developing lab for reprints before returning them to AP. When he returned to pick them up he was greeted by the East Lansing police. The police, who had been alerted by the staff of the photo shop about the content of the images, already had taken possession of the negatives and photographs. They detained McCreery for two hours until a search warrant could be obtained. The police then took all the film and permitted McCreery to leave.

The East Lansing police immediately posted the photographs on a "Hall of Shame" Web site and offered cash rewards of up to $50,000 for identification of "suspects." (The Web site is www.ci.east-lansing.mi.us/Riot/index.htm.) Many of the photographs showed acts of rioting but the mainstay simply contained photographs of people standing in groups — with the caption "wanted for incitement of riot." The police, moreover, placed a copyright notice on the Web site claiming ownership of the images.

The police then obtained subpoenas against 11 news organizations that were not so unlucky as to have their film turned over to police by cooperative photo processors. These subpoenas were opposed through motions to quash in the Michigan Circuit Court for the County of Ingham and the Michigan Supreme Court. The subpoenas ultimately failed not because of their First Amendment infirmity (which the parties and *amici* National Press Photographers Association argued) but because prosecutors did not use the correct procedures in obtaining them. McCreery was not so fortunate. Because his photographs were put into police possession before he could challenge the search warrant, he faced a difficult practical burden in getting them back and in stopping their publication on the East Lansing Web site.

Within days of the seizure, counsel for McCreery claimed in a demand letter that the City of Lansing had violated McCreery's First Amendment rights by seizing the film, and had violated the Copyright Act by publishing the photographs on its Web site and by claiming on the site that it owned the copyright to them. (The city also altered the photographs by blocking partial nudity on suspects "wanted for indecent exposure" and by placing "IDENTIFIED!" banners across the pictures of some suspects.) The city not only refused to take the Web site down, but in fact began running McCreery's photographs on its government access cable television channel in East Lansing.

Counsel for McCreery made a parallel demand under the Digital Millennium Copyright Act of 1998 to the Internet service provider hosting the City of Lansing's site, alleging that the ISP would be liable for copyright infringement for hosting the site if it did not take the site down until the copyright dispute was resolved. The ISP did agree to take down the Web site but the city council of East Lansing voted, remarkably, to indemnify the ISP against any copyright liability. At the end of 1999, the site was still active and still displayed McCreery's photographs. Numerous suspects have been identified using the East Lansing Web site.

Woodstock, N.Y.

This "success" by law enforcement set the scene for New York State police to post photographs taken by photojournalists of the melee at the historic Woodstock '99 rock concert, using an Internet site established to identify suspects. Following the concert in late July, the New York State Troopers Web site posted 14 photographs of suspects engaged in alleged rioting and looting (www.troopers.state.ny.us). Ten of these photos were taken by Associated Press photographers and were used without permission. Others were obtained from the Web sites of Syracuse Newspapers group and other newspapers — police simply downloaded the photographs and reposted them on the troopers' Web site.

The Associated Press, supported by a variety of New York associations and media outlets, demanded to the State Police and to Gov. George Pataki that the photographs be taken down. The AP raised First Amendment issues in addition to claiming that its copyright interest in the photographs had been infringed by the activities of the troopers. State police rejected AP's demands and told the press that about 40 e-mails potentially identifying suspects had been received. The chief counsel for the State Police, Glenn Valle, took the remarkable position that there was no infringement in its publication of the photographs because "it was material that was already published."

On Aug. 10, 1999, the State Police relented and removed the AP photographs from the Web site. Police representatives maintained that no First Amendment or copyright issues required the photographs to be taken down, but claimed that the photographs had been removed because they "didn't provide any more leads." No arrests have been attributed specifically to the Web site, although about 150 e-mail responses were received and 39 people arrested overall.

— Kurt Wimmer

J. Food Lion Reversal Looks Like Media Victory but Spells Trouble for Investigative Reporting

Taken at face value, the decision of the U.S. Court of Appeals for the Fourth Circuit in *Food Lion, Inc. v. Capital Cities/ABC, Inc.*, 194 F.3d 505 (4th Cir. 1999), appears to be a victory for the press. Damages were reduced for a second time after a jury awarded Food Lion over $5.5 million in compensatory and punitive damages for newsgathering torts committed by ABC. However, beneath the surface lies trouble for the future of investigative journalism.

Background

The case began in early 1992, when the producers of ABC's "PrimeTime Live" program received a report alleging that Food Lion stores were engaging in unsanitary meat handling practices. Reporters Lynne Dale and Susan Barnett were assigned to the story. With the approval of their supervisors, both applied for jobs with Food Lion. They submitted applications with false identities, references, education, employment history, and addresses — most notably omitting the reporters' current employment with ABC. Barnett was hired as a deli clerk in a South Carolina Food Lion store, where she worked for two weeks; Dale was hired as a meat wrapper in a North Carolina Food Lion store, where she worked for one week.

During the period of their employment, each reporter used hidden cameras and microphones to secretly record fellow employees treating, wrapping, and labeling meat and fish. Forty-five hours of footage were eventually recorded, some of which was used in a Nov. 5, 1992 broadcast of "PrimeTime Live." This videotape appeared to show employees repackaging and redating fish that had passed the expiration date, grinding expired beef with fresh beef, and applying barbecue sauce to expired chicken to mask its smell and sell it as fresh in the gourmet section. The truth of the broadcast was never an issue in litigation.

District Court Action

Food Lion filed suit in the U.S. District Court for the Middle District of North Carolina, asserting fraud, breach of the duty of loyalty, trespass, and unfair trade practices. It sought to recover compensatory damages for administrative costs and wages paid in connection with the employment of Dale and Barnett, and for loss of goodwill, lost sales and profits, and diminished stock value resulting from the broadcast itself (commonly known as "publication damages"). Food Lion also sought punitive damages.

The jury ruled in favor of Food Lion. It found ABC had engaged in fraud and had violated the North Carolina Unfair and Deceptive Trade Practices Act (NCUDTPA). The jury also found that the reporters were liable for breach of the duty of loyalty and trespass.

The district court ruled that damages incurred as a result of the actual "PrimeTime Live" broadcast could not be recovered because these were not proximately caused by ABC's acts. *Food Lion, Inc. v. Capital Cities/ABC, Inc.*, 964 F. Supp. 956, 958 (M.D.N.C. 1997). The jury then awarded Food Lion compensatory damages in the amount of $1,400 for fraud, $1 for breach of the duty of loyalty, $1 for trespass, and $1,500 for violation of the NCUDTPA. The jury also awarded Food Lion $5,545,750 in punitive damages on the fraud claim, which the district court reduced to $315,000 in a post-trial ruling. ABC's post-trial Motion for Judgment as a Matter of Law was denied.

Appeals to Fourth Circuit

Both sides appealed. ABC appealed the denial of its Motion for Judgment as a Matter of Law. Food Lion appealed the district court's ruling that Food Lion could not recover damages stemming from the broadcast itself.

The first issue on appeal was whether the defendants could be held liable for fraud, breach of the duty of loyalty, and trespass as a matter of North Carolina and South Carolina law, and whether the NCUDTPA applies. The court of appeals first addressed ABC's argument that the district court erred in upholding the $1,400 fraud verdict because Food Lion did not prove any injury was proximately caused by the actions of ABC reporters.

Fraud

There are four elements to a fraud claim under North Carolina law. The plaintiff must prove the defendant (1) made a misrepresentation of material fact; (2) knew the misrepresentation was false or made it with reckless disregard as to truth or falsity; (3) intended that the plaintiff rely upon it; and (4) injured the plaintiff when the plaintiff reasonably relied upon the false representation. The court of appeals noted the first three elements were undisputed; only the issue of injurious reliance was at issue.

Food Lion asserted two categories of injury. First, it incurred costs associated with hiring and training new employees. Second, Food Lion paid wages to reporters Dale and Barnett it would not have paid but for the reliance on their misrepresentations. The court of appeals disagreed with the alleged first injury, stating that these administrative costs would be associated with the hiring of any new employee — due to the high turnover in this line of work, had Food Lion not hired these employees it would have hired two other employees for which it would have incurred the same costs.

Food Lion also sought compensation for the wages paid to the reporters, alleging the reporters did not earn those wages. The court of appeals disagreed, noting the reporters were paid because they showed up for work and performed their assigned tasks as employees — even receiving favorable reviews from superiors. The court of appeals thus reversed the fraud verdict in favor of Food Lion.

Breach of the Duty of Loyalty

ABC also argued the reporters could not be held liable for breach of the duty of loyalty under North Carolina and South Carolina law. The jury had awarded $1 to Food Lion for this tort. The test for breach of the duty of loyalty under the laws of both states is similar: whether the employee engages in acts inconsistent with promoting the best interest of his or her employer at the time the employee is on the payroll. ABC's claim was premised on the fact that these issues are usually a contract matter and are not sued for in tort, except in three situations: (1) when an employee competes directly with his or her employer or company; (2) when an employee misappropriates the employer's profits, property, or business opportunities; or (3) when the employee breaches the employer's confidences.

The court of appeals upheld the district court's ruling that the reporters had breached the duty of loyalty to Food Lion. It found the reporters had given their loyalty to ABC at a time when the network's interests were averse to Food Lion; specifically, ABC desired to expose Food Lion for deceiving the public. The court of appeals held the tort required at least some amount of competition:

> In these circumstances, we believe that the highest courts of North Carolina and South Carolina would hold that the reporters — in promoting the interests of one master, ABC, to the detriment of a second, Food Lion — committed the tort of disloyalty against Food Lion.

> Our holding on this point is not a sweeping one. An employee does not commit a tort simply by holding two jobs or by performing a second job inadequately.... Because Dale and Barnett had the requisite intent to act against the interests of their second employer, Food Lion, for the benefit of their main employer, ABC, they were liable in tort for their disloyalty. *Food Lion*, 194 F.3d at 516.

Trespass

The court of appeals then tackled the trespass issue. ABC argued it was error to hold the defendants liable for trespass because Food Lion had consented to the reporters' presence in employee-only areas of the stores and this consent was not rendered void by the employees' misrepresentations. The court of appeals agreed, recognizing that consent is often obtained through misrepresentation — and that this misrepresentation is often necessary: "Without this result, a restaurant critic could not conceal his identity when he ordered a meal, or a browser pretend to be interested in merchandise he could not buy." *Id.* at 517.

While the court of appeals held that misrepresentation alone did not nullify the consent given to an employee to enter the employer's property, it did find that this consent was invalidated by the breach of the duty of loyalty. This is because both reporters became employees of Food Lion only with the knowledge that they would breach their implied promises to serve Food Lion faithfully. These promises gave them access to areas off limits to the public, access they used to directly harm the interests of their employer. The trespass verdict was thus sustained.

NCUDTPA

ABC also argued that no damages should stem from violations of the North Carolina Unfair and Deceptive Trade Practices Act. The court of appeals agreed. It noted that the Act's primary purpose is to protect the public and that a business may only assert a violation of the Act against another business when the two businesses are competitors or in dealings with one another. The court of appeals reversed this verdict against ABC.

ABC's First Amendment Defense

The second major issue tackled by the court of appeals was ABC's argument that the district court erred in not subjecting any of Food Lion's claims to First Amendment scrutiny. The court of appeals began its analysis by stating: "The Supreme Court has said in no uncertain terms that 'generally applicable laws do not offend the First Amendment simply because their enforcement against the press has incidental effects on its ability to gather and report the news.'" *Food Lion*, 194 F.3d at 520 (citing *Cohen v. Cowles Media Co.*, 501 U.S. 663, 669 (1991)).

The court of appeals believed the present case fit neatly into the *Cowles* framework. None of the torts involved singled out the press. The torts simply applied to daily transactions undertaken by citizens of each state. Nor did the court of appeals believe that application of these torts would have more than an incidental effect on the press: "We are convinced that the media can do its important job effectively without resort to run-of-the-mill torts." *Food Lion*, 194 F.3d at 521. The court of appeals ruled that ABC was not entitled to any protection through heightened First Amendment scrutiny of its newsgathering activities.

Consideration of Publication Damages

The last issue taken up by the court of appeals was Food Lion's appeal from the denial of publication damages — those damages stemming from the broadcast itself. The court cited to *Hustler Magazine v. Falwell*, 485 U.S. 46 (1988), for the proposition that a plaintiff may not seek to avoid First Amendment limitations on defamation claims simply by seeking publication damages on other tort claims. Essentially, Food Lion, knowing that it had no valid defamation claim, sought an end run around the First Amendment by claiming that the newsgathering torts caused damages after publication — exactly the type of claim foreclosed by *Hustler*:

> *Hustler* confirms that when a public figure plaintiff uses a law to seek damages resulting from speech covered by the First Amendment, the plaintiff must satisfy the proof standard of *New York Times*. Here, Food Lion was not prepared to meet this standard for publication damages under any of the claims it asserted. Unless there is some way to distinguish *Hustler* (we think there is not), Food Lion cannot sustain its request for publication damages from the ABC broadcast. *Food Lion*, 194 F.3d at 523.

The court of appeals reversed the judgment of the district court that ABC had committed fraud, and erased the $1,400 in compensatory damages and $315,000 in punitive damages owed on that claim. It affirmed the judgment to the extent it provided that Dale and Barnett had breached their duty of loyalty to Food Lion and committed a trespass, awarding $1 in damages on each claim.

Despite the reduction of the original damages from over $5.5 million to $2, this decision is not a wholesale victory for the press. The reinforcement of *Cowles* means that the press must once again examine closely its newsgathering practices without the benefit of extra protection from the First Amendment. More important are the holdings with regard to the breach of the duty of loyalty and trespass. While generally lauding the role of the undercover journalist, the Fourth Circuit opinion appears to take away any ability for reporters to engage in this practice, as the opinion appears to require that the reporter divulge his or her true identity during the application process.

— **Richard M. Schmidt, Jr. and Kevin M. Goldberg**

D+

K. Avis Seeks High Court Review of Dubious California Judgment Enjoining Employee's Speech

Once in a while a judicial assault on free expression comes along that does not involve media parties but nevertheless has serious implications for the communications media. Such a case is *Aguilar v. Avis Rent A Car System, Inc.,* 21 Cal. 4th 121, 87 Cal. Rptr. 2d 132, 980 P.2d 846 (Cal. 1999). There, a jury found that a rental car company had engaged in employment discrimination, in part by permitting plaintiffs, all Hispanics, to be the target of racial epithets repeatedly mouthed by a fellow employee. In addition to awarding damages, the trial court issued an injunction prohibiting the offending employee from using such epithets in the future and requiring the company to police the employee.

Prior Restraint?

The defendants argued first in the intermediate appellate court and then in the California Supreme Court that such an injunction was an unconstitutional prior restraint of their speech. The court of appeal reversed the injunctive portion of the judgment and ordered the trial court to limit its scope to the workplace only. Further, to avoid vagueness, the court ordered the trial court to add "an exemplary list" of prohibited derogatory racial or ethnic epithets, such as those actually used in the workplace in the case. The California Supreme Court granted review and in a plurality opinion affirmed the judgment of the lower appellate court.

At the outset of his opinion, concurred in by only two other justices (a third concurred in the judgment), Chief Justice George cited *Near v. Minnesota*, 283 U.S. 697 (1931). But he showed not the slightest understanding of the thrust of that venerable case, *i.e.*, the need in a democratic society for free expression. 87 Cal. Rptr. 2d at 141, 980 P.2d at 853. The chief justice stated flatly that "[u]nder well established law ... the injunction at issue is not an invalid prior restraint, because the order was issued only after the jury determined that defendants had engaged in employment discrimination, and the order simply precluded defendants from continuing their unlawful activity." 87 Cal. Rptr. 2d at 144, 980 P.2d at 856-57.

Thus, according to the chief justice, if a jury finds a certain speech to be in violation of state legislation such as the California Fair Employment and Housing Act (the statute involved in the case), enjoining such speech is not an unconstitutional prior restraint under either the state or federal constitution.

Four California Justices Dissent

No critiques by outside commentators are needed here because insightful criticism of this dubious opinion is provided by four of Chief Justice George's own judicial colleagues. Justice Werdegar, who concurred only in the judgment of the court (87 Cal. Rptr. 2d at 152, 980 P.2d at 863), wrote:

> To the extent the plurality opinion affirms the judgment of the Court of Appeal, and with my understanding of the purpose and context of the "exemplary list" of words ... I concur. I write separately because the plurality opinion does not address what I believe to be a critical preliminary question, that is, whether the First Amendment permits imposition of civil liability under FEHA for pure speech that creates a racially hostile or abusive work environment. By declining to address this question, the plurality opinion fails to acknowledge that we are with this case sailing into uncharted First Amendment waters. No decision by the United States Supreme Court has, as yet, declared that the First Amendment permits restrictions on speech creating a hostile work environment....

She answered that critical question in the affirmative because of her belief that, arguably, when employees are forced to endure racially harassing speech on the job substantial privacy interests are being invaded in an intolerable manner, and that without injunctive relief they cannot be protected against unwanted racial discrimination. (Although she forgets, perhaps, that the award of money damages may cause bigots to think twice before uttering hateful words.)

Justice Mosk, the most senior member of the court, dissented and wrote:

> According to the Chief Justice, the injunction passes constitutional muster because it simply precludes defendants from continuing their unlawful activity. It does more than that. It directly targets otherwise protected speech, forbidding any future use of a list of offensive words in the workplace — even outside the presence of plaintiffs and even if welcome or overtly permitted. Although the lead opinion insists that it would prohibit an illegal course of conduct, in fact it regulates speech on the basis of expressive content. 87 Cal. Rptr. 2d at 169, 980 P.2d at 879.

Justice Kennard also dissented and criticized the plurality decision, though on narrower grounds. She believed the injunction to be invalid under the free speech guarantees of both the federal and state constitutions because the record failed to establish that an injunction restricting future speech was necessary to prevent a recurrence of the employment discrimination, and because it was not drawn narrowly enough to target only that prohibited discrimination. 87 Cal. Rptr. 2d at 173, 980 P.2d at 882.

The most ringing rejection of the plurality opinion came from Justice Brown:

> If there is a bedrock principle underlying the First Amendment, it is that the government may not prohibit the expression of an idea simply because society finds the idea itself offensive or disagreeable" (*Texas v. Johnson* (1989) 491 U.S. 397, 414, 109 S. Ct. 2533, 105 L. Ed. 2d 342) — that is, until today. Today, this court holds that an idea that happens to offend someone in the workplace is "not constitutionally protected." (Plur. opn., *ante*, 87 Cal. Rptr. 2d at p. 144, 980 P.2d at p. 856.) Why? Because it creates a "hostile ... work environment" (*id.* at p. 135, 980 P.2d at p. 848) in violation of the Fair Employment and Housing Act (FEHA).... In essence, the court has recognized the FEHA exception to the First Amendment. 87 Cal. Rptr. 2d at 182, 980 P.2d at 890.

Continuing, Justice Brown stated:

> The plurality repeatedly asserts that the prior restraint at issue here is permitted under the First Amendment "because defendants simply were enjoined from continuing a course of repetitive speech that had been judicially determined to constitute unlawful harassment in violation of the FEHA." (Plur. opn., *ante*, 87 Cal. Rptr. 2d at 149-150, 980 P.2d at 861 (additional citations omitted).) So speech that is "unlawful" is now unprotected by the state and federal Constitutions. That standard turns the world on its head. In effect, the plurality says, "The Legislature, acting in response to current popular sentiments, has carved out certain ideas from the universe of ideas and declared them to be bad ideas, and once an idea has been judicially determined to be one of these bad ideas, courts can prohibit anyone from expressing it." I disagree. 87 Cal. Rptr. 2d at 185, 980 P.2d at 893.

And finally, Justice Brown pointed out the philosophical blindness of the plurality opinion when she wrote:

> Fundamentally, this is a case about equality and freedom. Thus, it is a case about our most basic political ideals; about our highest aspirations and our greatest failures; our toughest challenges and our deepest fears. It is about a bafflingly elusive dream of equality and the freedom, not immune from abuse, to speak words that make others more than uncomfortable. It is a case about equality and freedom and the irreconcilable tension between the two. We are all the

beneficiaries of the freedom the Constitution guarantees, and we all pay its costs, even though the price may sometimes be anguish. 87 Cal. Rptr. 2d at 187, 980 P.2d at 895.

To Avis Rent A Car's great credit, it has pursued its prior restraint claim through the entire California judicial system and has now petitioned for a writ of *certiorari* from the U.S. Supreme Court (see *U.S. Law Week* 3327, Nov. 1, 1999 (Sup. Ct. No. 99-781)). It can only be hoped that the Court will take the case and reverse the California Supreme Court's judgment, thus eliminating any precedential value the state court's plurality judgment and opinion may have.

— **Harvey L. Zuckman**

L. Revised 'Son of Sam' Laws Now Being Put to the Test

Developments in California and elsewhere during 1999 have launched new challenges to so-called "Son of Sam" laws. Nearly all states have such measures. They take their name from a New York law from the late '70s enacted to keep serial killer David Berkowitz from making money by telling the story of his crimes.

The New York law covered anyone accused of a crime, not just those tried and convicted, and prohibited even minor references to the crime in a book or other work. The law required that an "entity" contracting with anyone suspected of or convicted of a crime had to put the money due the person in an escrow account with the state Crime Victims Board. Any victim who, within five years, obtained a civil judgment against the person accused or convicted could receive the money.

After the U.S. Supreme Court struck down the New York law on First Amendment grounds in 1991, most states revised their laws to cover only convicted criminals and works that focused on a particular crime, rather than just mentioning it.

New Challenges to Son of Sam Laws

In California, where the Son of Sam law applies to all income from any product if the criminal's notoriety has enhanced the value, a legal battle over whether a convicted kidnapper can make a movie deal seems the most likely to test the revised law's constitutionality.

In December 1998, the California Supreme Court agreed to review the case of Barry Kennan, who served four years (reduced from an original life sentence) for the kidnapping of Frank Sinatra Jr. in 1963. When it became known that Kennan had made a $1.5-million deal with Columbia Pictures for a movie called "Snatching Sinatra," the kidnapping victim went to court and won a court order preventing the movie studio from paying Kennan. Now a successful real estate developer, Kennan says the law violates his First Amendment right to tell his story. After losing in the lower courts, Kennan has taken his case to the state's highest court with the backing of the Southern California chapter of the American Civil Liberties Union.

Concerned that the courts might not uphold the California law, relatives of three women murdered in Yosemite National Park last summer have sued Cary Stayner, the man who confessed to the slayings, for any proceeds he might realize from selling his story.

Also last December, the First District Court of Appeal in Florida rejected an appeal by Sondra London, who has made a national reputation as a free-lance writer with her interviews and profiles of serial killers. London was fighting a lower court order to turn over $15,000 in money she made on articles she wrote about killer Danny Rolling, who killed five coeds at the University of Florida. Rolling did not get any of the money. London has vowed to continue her legal fight.

In Washington State in September 1999, the attorney for Mary K. Letourneau, the teacher serving time for child rape because of her relationship with one of her students, argued before the state court of appeals that Letourneau had a constitutional right to profits from movie or book deals. The 1993 law does not prevent Letourneau from writing or speaking about the crime but she cannot profit from it. Perhaps anticipating a challenge to the law, the judge in sentencing Letourneau also prohibited her from profiting from books and other works. One book about her crime already has been published in France, a locally written book has been translated into 11 languages, and a television movie made in Canada already has aired on USA Network.

Jurisprudence

The U.S. Supreme Court has ruled on the Son of Sam laws only once. In 1991, New York's law was struck down in *Simon & Schuster v. New York State Crime Victims Board*, 502 U.S. 105 (1991). In that case, the publishing company had contracted with organized crime figure Henry Hill for a book about his life. The Crime Victims Board ordered the publisher to turn over money Hill was supposed to be paid. Simon & Schuster sued, claiming the law violated the First Amendment.

The district court found no constitutional problem with the law and the court of appeals affirmed that decision. But the Supreme Court overturned in an 8-to-0 opinion written by Justice O'Connor. The Court said the law was too broad and would violate the First Amendment regardless of whether it was the speech of the publisher or the prisoner.

In 1995, California Attorney General Dan Lungren filed two Son of Sam actions. One was against Joe Hunt, the "Billionaire Boys Club" killer who had set up a 900 number to discuss prison life. The state eventually dropped the case. In the second suit, the state sued to recover money to be paid by a television show to Richard Allen Davis, convicted of killing 12-year-old Polly Klaas. Because investigators were unable to track the money, the case was put on hold and is likely to be dropped.

Possible Challenges

A new generation of Son of Sam-type laws may be provoked by creative modes of communication developed by prisoners and the media.

In September 1999, New York prison authorities revoked the arts and crafts privileges of Arthur Shawcross, serving life for killing 11 women in the Rochester area, after his artwork was offered for sale on the eBay Internet auction site. Shawcross did not receive money for the items; instead, he received gifts of clothes and shoes. He is charged specifically with running a business from the prison rather than violating the Son of Sam law, since he did not profit from the sales. But New York Sen. Michael Nozzolio wants to broaden the law to cover such activity.

The New York case and the growing presence of prisoner collectibles offered for sale on the Internet and elsewhere have legislators in Texas calling for similar legislation. Texas does not have a Son of Sam law.

California Attorney General Bill Lockyer filed a Son of Sam lawsuit in May 1999 to recover proceeds from the sale of a rap album made by inmate Anerae Brown, a convicted murderer, inside prison walls. The CD does not refer specifically to the 1992 killing of Patricia Harris, but it does contain "murderous images," the attorney general charged.

California officials also are looking at applying the Son of Sam law to a new series of adult videos that feature women convicted of crime. *Hustler* magazine publisher Larry Flynt produced the series, called "Jail Babes." Asked whether the appearances of the convicted criminals in the videos violated the Son of Sam law, California Deputy Attorney General Peter Shack said he would look into it. In an interview with the *Los Angeles Times*, law professor Robert Pugsley said he believed the fees paid the convict-actors are subject to the law.

First Amendment Concerns

Civil liberties advocates will be watching these cases with great interest because of First Amendment implications. There is a great public appetite for crime stories, whether in film or print form. Opponents of Son of Sam laws say that movie makers, television producers, book publishers, researchers, and scholars all have a right to tap that interest and to inform public discourse. They say the laws could prevent works such as *Civil Disobedience* by Henry David Thoreau, *The Autobiography of Malcolm X*, *Soul on Ice* by Eldridge Cleaver, or *Cell 2455: Death Row* by Caryl Chessman. Son of Sam laws also implicate the free speech rights of persons convicted of crimes, as well as the rights of ordinary citizens to receive such information, whether for entertainment purposes or to participate in an informed public policy debate.

— Paul K. McMasters

Profiles of the Contributors

Robert Corn-Revere is a partner in the Washington, D.C., office of Hogan & Hartson LLP, specializing in First Amendment and communications law. He was a legal advisor to former FCC commissioner James H. Quello, and a former chief counsel of the Commission. He teaches at the Institute for Communications Law Studies at the Columbus School of Law, Catholic University of America.

Kevin M. Goldberg is an associate with the firm of Cohn and Marks in Washington, D.C., who specializes in First Amendment and constitutional law issues. He received his J.D. with High Honors from The George Washington University National Law Center in 1995, where he was also the recipient of the Imogene Williford Constitutional Law Award.

Margaret A. Gorzkowski is an associate with the intellectual property firm Finnegan, Henderson, Farabow, Garrett & Dunner, LLP. She specializes in trademark and copyright law. Prior to joining the firm, Ms. Gorzkowski served as the Legal Research Associate in the office of the First Amendment Ombudsman at The Freedom Forum.

David L. Hudson, Jr. is an attorney with the First Amendment Center at Vanderbilt University, funded by The Freedom Forum. He focuses on commercial speech, hate speech, obscenity/indeceny, and cyberlibel. In addition to writing for The Freedom Forum's online news service, he regularly contributes to *Commercial Speech Digest* and the American Bar Association's *Preview of United States Supreme Court Cases*.

Paul K. McMasters is the First Amendment Ombudsman of The Freedom Forum in Arlington, Va. A 32-year veteran of journalism, he served previously as executive director of The Freedom Forum First Amendment Center and as associate editorial director of *USA Today*. He is a former national president of the Society of Professional Journalists.

Robert M. O'Neil has, since 1990, been Founding Director of The Thomas Jefferson Center for the Protection of Free Expression in Charlottesville. He is also a professor of law at the University of Virginia, where he teaches courses in free speech and press, including seminars on First Amendment and the arts and free expression in cyberspace.

Judith Platt is Director of Communications and Public Affairs and Director of the Freedom To Read Program at the Association of American Publishers in Washington. She is responsible for articulating the views of the U.S. book publishing industry on free speech issues and opposing attempts to undermine First Amendment rights. She is a Trustee of the ALA-affiliated Freedom To Read Foundation.

Richard M. Schmidt, Jr. has served as general counsel of the American Society of Newspaper Editors, and Washington counsel for The Association of American Publishers, Inc., since 1969. Of counsel to the Washington, D.C., law firm of Cohn and Marks, Mr. Schmidt is a member of the Board of Trustees of the National Press Foundation.

Rodney A. Smolla is the George Allen Professor of Law at the T.C. Williams School of Law, University of Richmond. Previously he was a law professor and director of the Institute of Bill of Rights Law at the College of William and Mary. A graduate of Yale University and Duke Law School, he has authored a casebook on the First Amendment, three treatises, and several other books. He also has co-authored a casebook on constitutional law.

Daniel E. Troy specializes in constitutional and appellate litigation at the Washington, D.C., firm of Wiley, Rein & Fielding. He is also an associate scholar of legal studies at the American Enterprise Institute. Mr. Troy has published widely on the subject of commercial speech and on other constitutional issues.

Kurt Wimmer is a partner in the Washington, D.C., office of Covington and Burling, where he focuses on media, telecommunications, and Internet law. He chairs the firm's Information Technology and Internet Practice Group, representing new media, television, online services, and new telecommunications providers. He is also chair of the Libel Defense Resource Center's Cyberspace Committee.

Laurence H. Winer is a professor of law and Faculty Fellow of the Center for the Study of Law, Science and Technology at Arizona State University College of Law. He specializes in media law, constitutional law, and legal ethics. Prof. Winer received his B.A., M.A., and Ph.D. (all in mathematics) from Boston University, and received his law degree from Yale Law School. He is a former editor in chief of the *Jurimetrics Journal of Law, Science and Technology*.

Harvey L. Zuckman is Director of The Institute for Communications Law Studies at The Catholic University of America in Washington, D.C. He is a professor of law at the university's Columbus School of Law, and has written extensively on First Amendment and media law subjects. Prof. Zuckman is the co-author of *Modern Communication Law*, a multi-volume treatise, and *Mass Communications Law*, a widely used student text.

The Editor: **Richard T. Kaplar** is Vice President of The Media Institute in Washington, D.C. He has written, edited, or produced over 35 books and monographs on a variety of First Amendment and communications policy topics. Mr. Kaplar is the author of *Advertising Rights: The Neglected Freedom*, and co-author of *The Government Factor: Undermining Journalistic Ethics in the Information Age*.

The Media Institute

The Media Institute is a nonprofit research foundation specializing in communications policy and First Amendment issues. The Institute exists to advocate and encourage freedom of speech, a competitive communications industry, and excellence in journalism.

Founded in 1979, The Media Institute pursues a program agenda that encompasses virtually all sectors of the media, ranging from traditional print and broadcast outlets to contemporary entrants such as satellite broadcasters and the Internet.

The Institute publishes books and monographs, prepares regulatory filings and court briefs, convenes conferences, and sponsors a luncheon series in Washington for journalists and communications executives.

Since its inception, the Institute has been an independent advocate of a robust press and a dynamic communications industry. The organization has evolved into one of the country's leading "think tanks" focusing on the First Amendment and communications policy.

To support the work of the Institute, or for further information, contact Patrick D. Maines, President, The Media Institute, Suite 301, 1000 Potomac Street, N.W., Washington, D.C. 20007.

The First Amendment and the Media - 2000 was produced by Nikolaos Beratlis.
Cover design: Cameron Falkenhagen
Digital imagery ©1999 PhotoDisc, Inc.